W9-AHU-268

The Gentle Art
of Communicating
with Kids

The Gentle Art of Communicating with Kids

---◆---

Suzette Haden Elgin, Ph.D.

John Wiley & Sons, Inc.

New York • Chichester • Brisbane • Toronto • Singapore

This text is printed on acid-free paper.

Copyright © 1996 by Suzette Haden Elgin, Ph.D.
Published by John Wiley & Sons, Inc.

Library of Congress Cataloging-in-Publication Data
Elgin, Suzette Haden.
   The gentle art of communicating with kids / Suzette Haden Elgin
      p.   cm.
   Includes bibliographical references and index.
      ISBN 0-471-03973-X (alk. paper). --ISBN 0-471-03996-9 (pbk. :
alk. paper)

Printed in the United States of America

10   9   8   7   6   5   4   3   2   1

Contents

Preface

My parents and teachers used to look at me in total exasperation and say, "Talking to you is like talking to my ELbow!" When I grew old enough, I started saying back, "Well, talking to *you* is like talking to a WALL!" They had exchanged those same lines with *their* parents; I've exchanged them with my children and grandchildren as well. The way this sort of interaction spans the generations might suggest that we adults who want good communication with children can relax. Maybe we only need to be sure we're comfortable with the latest slang and computer terms, and we can otherwise rely on the same tactics our grandparents used.

Maybe — but I don't think so. Let's look at something Nick Gillespie had to say about this subject in the December 1994 issue of *Reason:*

> I've come to realize that as a parent you view the world of your child through the eyes of a stranger in a strange land. Even as you attempt to guide and protect your charge . . . you realize that you do not really speak the language, know the rituals, or comprehend the customs of the world in which your child will live. It is flush with dangers — and opportunities — that you never encountered. . . . Unfortunately, most of what you learned growing up is by necessity outdated, outmoded, and obsolete.

This was always true, wasn't it? And we always managed to raise our kids successfully all the same. This isn't *news*. Right? Not exactly.

Every adult has once in a while tried to communicate with a youngster and ended up thinking, "This kid must have been dropped out of the sky at birth by Giant Alien Beings! This kid must have been switched in the cradle for the human child I was *supposed* to get! We have *nothing* in common, this child and I! *Zero!*" Probably this was true even before cradles, in the days when the major hazards a family faced were sabertooth tigers and drafty caves. *But only rarely in human history has Nick Gillespie's statement been true the way it's true today.*

The most recent example we have of such a situation is that point in history when adults who'd always lived in an illiterate society—where only the elite could read, and books were priceless treasures—suddenly had to communicate with youngsters who took both books and reading for granted. We are smack in the middle of a change like *that* one today, for the first time in more than a thousand years.

When television came into our homes, it didn't bring this kind of revolutionary change with it. Parents hadn't grown up with TV, but they *did* grow up with movies and radios. That gave them a bridge they could fling across the generation gap. TV was just a movie in your home, just radio with pictures; it wasn't a whole new and foreign reality. This kind of change didn't happen when computers arrived in our homes and schools, either. The computers were enough like typewriters to provide the same sort of communication bridge.

The revolution *has* happened now, however. It's here, and it's too late to go back. It came with the arrival of virtual reality—*reality that doesn't have to have a physical location in space.* It came with the arrival of remote controls—innocent-looking little gadgets that let our youngsters grow up channel-surfing, truly able to watch three or four different programs at the same time and follow them *all*, something we adults aren't able to do. It came with music videos, which tell stories in an entirely new way that isn't based on a beginning, and then a middle, and then an end. Suddenly the children are out cruising the information highway while the grownups are still on the back roads. And unlike the situation with television sets and computers, we can't link up the generations just by learning a new vocabulary. The change is bigger than that, and the consequences of ignoring it are a lot more serious than they were for those smaller changes.

Adults today have to be able to talk to children for whom "Where were you last night?" is a silly question, because the only "where" involved is inside their computers, in cyberspace.

They have to able to talk to kids for whom the whole idea of schedules is radically different (and often irrelevant) because when the kids are in a meeting and are needed somewhere else, they can just open a window on their screen and be in both of those "places" at the same time. And they can do that *easily*. It doesn't bother them; it doesn't seem strange or difficult.

Today's parents have to be able to discuss homework with children for whom it's not true that every kid in the class works from the same book. These kids have hypertexts to work with, and every path they take through a hypertext gives them a *unique* book that no other child has except by chance.

Adults have to be able to communicate with kids like the little girl Richard Wolkomir writes about in "We're Going to Have Computers Coming Out of the Woodwork" in the September 1994 *Smithsonian Magazine.* She was visiting Xerox Corporation with her parents when, as if by magic, messages for the adults started appearing on a new gadget Xerox calls a "Liveboard." "The guests looked dumbfounded," Wolkomir tells us, "but the child blithely scribbled messages back." From the child's point of view, why *shouldn't* personal messages materialize seemingly out of nowhere on a blank surface? That kind of thing is no problem for today's children, who are often as familiar with "nowhere" as they are with their bedrooms.

This shift can't be handled by learning a list of new words and phrases. It's a *radically* new way of living in the world and relating to it and interacting with it, where even the words we thought were most stable — even words like "time" and "space" — now mean something very different from what they used to mean.

I know what you're thinking, because I've been there. I've thought that. I understand. I've raised four children (plus a stepchild who was sometimes in my home and sometimes elsewhere), often in very difficult circumstances. I'm actively involved in raising seven of my nine grandchildren, and I spend a lot of time trying to find ways to stay in touch with the other two, who live on the other side of the world. I've taught children at every level of the educational system from preschool to graduate school. I've counseled children for every kind of problem from the "I can't tie a bow" kind to pregnancies and bankruptcies and matters of life and death. I can understand why you might be thinking something roughly like this:

> Here I am trying to figure out how to get my kids to chew with their mouths shut, and you're coming at me with all that stuff about virtual realities and information highways! I'll get to that *later*. Just tell me how to make them chew with their mouths shut!

I'm sorry; I really am. But you can't afford to take that position. Reasonable as it seems, sensible as it used to be, tempting as it still is, you can't afford it. Not any more. Not if you'd like to have any chance to enjoy what are called your "Golden Years." Not if you'd like your children to be happy and successful adults.

Because children who don't learn to function well in this new and different world are going to need substantial help from you as long as they live. Because children whose caregivers don't equip them to join the information revolution are going to be severely handicapped when they try to compete with those who've learned to be at ease there.

Already we hear horror stories about "boomerang" kids, who leave home (the same way you left home, somewhere around the age of twenty) but come right back when they discover that they're not *ready* to function out in the world. (Not to mention the many homes where the problem isn't the "empty nest" we've always thought we had to worry about, but the nest that is *full* with the children and the grandchildren.) It's not just that the rules have changed: *This is a whole new game.* And here is what that means for communication between adults and children:

✦ The *way* you go about persuading your kids to do such things as chewing with their mouths shut and carrying the cat right side up is *directly* linked to the way they will function as adults in a world you never imagined.

This doesn't mean matters are hopeless. It doesn't mean you should give up in despair. It doesn't mean you have to go take crash courses in all these new developments, many of which you don't have time for and aren't interested in. It *does* mean that you need to think about communication with youngsters in ways that may be completely new to you. It means you have to take a new *approach* to the use of language between adults and children. It means abandoning some myths that you may well cherish; it means becoming familiar with some truths that you may find unpleasant. But it's something you *can do.*

You started doing it when you gritted your teeth and kept on reading, even after noticing that I wasn't writing about how to keep the peanut butter side of the bread off your rug. And that's a good thing. Because not only your children's futures but your *own* future as well depend on it. You absolutely cannot afford to postpone or ignore it, even if the child you need to communicate with has only just said his or her first word.

Welcome to the new world that today's children have to live in — whether they like it or not. The world of cyberspace and hyperspace, cybertime and cyberkids. Today's youngsters, alien as they may seem, don't come from outer space. They do come from a whole new world that *coexists* with our adult world in very complicated ways.

Because adults are the *models* for children's behavior, there's only one way we can explore that world together, much less *live* in it together: We adults have to start acquiring the information and skills that *both* generations will need for communication. We have to fix it so that we *won't* be looking at the child's world through "the eyes of a stranger in a strange land."

We can do that, I promise you. It's not as easy as learning a list of "25 Words for Talking About Computers," but it's not all that hard, either. After all, we're in charge here; we have the advantages of wisdom and experience.

We're looking back now at a world where the generation that watched *Star Trek* could talk to the generation that watched *Wagon Train* because (as its author himself said) "Star Trek is only Wagon Train in space." The question now is what comes *after Star Trek,* and whether saying that it's "only *Star Trek* in hyperspace — only *Wagon Train* in cyberspace" will be enough.

What matters isn't being able to *predict* the future; that's not possible. What matters is equipping yourself, and the children you have responsibility for, to *deal* with that future when it's suddenly right there in your living room and in your classroom and at your dinner table. I'm going to tell you how you can do that.

Defining Our Terms

The easy way to do this would be for all of us just to go sit down together somewhere with coffee and doughnuts and talk it through. Since we don't have that option and we're going to do it with me as writer and you as reader, let's start by making sure that we all have shared definitions for five terms that we'll be needing as we go along:

1. Children

2. Language

3. The language environment

4. Language interaction

5. Utterance

Children. Confusion about how, exactly, to define "children" is hard to avoid. Today we even talk about "adult" children! I'll do two things to keep the confusion to a minimum. First, when the exact age or stage of childhood matters, I'll specify it. I'll say "a child of ten" or "a teenager" or "two sixteen-year-old children." (When gender matters, I'll specify that, too.) When all I need is a cover term for "nonadult," I'll say "youngster." Second, I'll assume throughout the book that childhood lasts from birth to age twenty, while adulthood lasts from age twenty until death. That's not always exactly accurate, but it's close enough, and it's clear.

Language. Language is much more than just words or signs. It's also body language, and body language is more than just gestures and postures and facial expressions. Body language includes the pitch and tone and rhythm of the voice (called *intonation.*) Language includes *silence,* which carries powerful messages. It includes the way people arrange themselves in space, as well as their choices of things to wear or carry with them. In this book we'll be focusing on words and intonation, but it's important always to remember this definition: *Language is anything a human being does that transmits a message.*

The Language Environment. There isn't any linguistic environmental movement, but there should be. We human beings took our *physical* environment for granted until very recently, and we're paying a high price for that neglect now. We've hardly begun to come to grips with the fact that there's also a *language* environment, and that abusive language is just another kind of pollution. We wouldn't let toxic chemicals or spoiled food pile up around us in our homes and schools and workplaces; it's just as unwise to live surrounded by toxic language. Fortunately, we don't have to. We are well equipped to keep our language environment safe and wholesome.

Language Interactions. We divide up all the kinds of talking human beings do with other human beings and give them names, like *conversations* and *interviews* and *interrogations* and so on. Often a particular one won't fit neatly under any label; it may be part conversation and part lecture and part interrogation and part something else entirely. *Language interaction* is a cover term for all those different kinds of communication events.

Utterance. Finally, we need the word "utterance," to cover all the words and body language a given person uses in a single *chunk* during a language interaction. People don't talk in paragraphs; often they don't talk in sentences. They talk in utterances.

How to Use This Book

The introduction will explain why good communication is so important today and will introduce the basic concepts we need for looking at communication in a new way, suitable for this new world we find ourselves in. Chapters 1 through 5 will explain five simple and practical language techniques that adults can put to immediate use to improve their communication with children. Chapter 6 takes up a set of special problems that adults today may have to face when communicating with youngsters, such as talking with a child who is suicidal, a child who is pregnant, or a child who is addicted to a drug. Chapter 7 is a brief review and summary. Next comes a series of Additional Resources, followed by a bibliography and an index for your reference. You'll find two kinds of help in the Additional Resources:

1. Descriptions of resources you can go to for more detailed information.

2. A brief overview of the *Gentle Art of Verbal Self-Defense* (the system this book is based on.)

There are two ways to use this book. You can just start at the beginning and read it straight through. Or, if you'd rather, you can go first to the Overview on pages 171–179 for a brief introduction to the system the book is based on before reading it through.

When we come to the end of this book, we will have discussed and analyzed many different cross-generation language interactions, from the primitive "NO! WON'T!" efforts of toddlers to the sophisticated tactics of youngsters in their late teens. I will have shown you ways to communicate with the younger generation successfully, without either compromising your own principles or using verbal abuse. You will have gained a solid foundation of valid information about language, and about the way language is learned and used. You'll be able to build on that foundation and use it to judge the distortions about the subject that appear in the mass media and elsewhere. Your knowledge of the grammar of verbal violence will be indexed and stored in your memory in a way that lets you get at it easily and use it with skill. And you'll be equipped with a set of techniques for keeping verbal abuse to the barest of minimums in your own language environment.

There are of course an infinite number of cross-generation communication situations and language interactions that won't even be mentioned. That is the nature of the object we call *a book:* Its contents are limited to what will fit between its covers. But even if we put it on a computer instead of on paper, we could never cover every potential communication problem. One of the things that *defines* real languages is that they're *infinite*; they can't be listed the way a code or a set of signals can.

But that's all right. Because when you finish the book what you will have available to you is a coherent *system* for dealing with all the rest of the language encounters that come your way. All its parts will fit together and interact to reinforce its strength and integrity.

You won't just have learned a set of tips to use when you talk with children or responses to use in a closed set of specific situations. You'll have learned a system of principles and techniques that you can rely on and that apply to every human communication situation, no matter how new and different. It's like learning to drive: Once you have it mastered, you can drive anywhere there's a road, even if you've never been on that road before. You may make mistakes on new routes and you may run into new problems and dangers, but you know the system — you can figure out how to manage.

Finally, you will have learned that you can *trust* your internal grammar, where all this information is now stored and classified and organized for your convenience.

Let's begin.

Introduction

Finding the On Ramp

How many times have you picked up a newspaper or turned on the news and come upon a story like this one?

> Family and neighbors are stunned and griefstricken tonight after learning that fifteen-year-old Tracy Jones killed herself sometime earlier today . . . [Or was arrested and charged with possession of cocaine . . . Or has run away from home and is now the subject of a nationwide search . . .] When Tracy's parents were interviewed, they talked to reporters through tears, saying, *"We just can't beLIEVE it! We never had the slightest hint that there was ANYthing WRONG!"*

And how many times have you asked yourself: When a youngster was in such desperate trouble, how could it possibly be true that the parents never even suspected that there was a problem?

Tragedies like this happen only when communication between the adults and children involved is so flawed that it's either useless or has broken down completely. Fortunately, this doesn't happen overnight; it takes a while. Toddlers don't commit suicide; five-year-olds don't sell drugs. Parents have quite a few years during which they can establish the kind of solid foundation for communication that will head off such disasters. Not that their children won't have problems. Having problems is part of being human. But they will be able to *talk* about them together and work together to solve them.

1

✦ We have to remember, however, that one of the characteristics of today's new world is that the age when crime and suicide and other such catastrophes begin is coming earlier and earlier in life. We're now dealing with these problems in elementary school, not just high school and beyond. We have less and less time to lay the groundwork.

We can't build that indispensable solid foundation for communication by heading straight out onto the information highway and trying to catch up with the kids. This is one of those times when haste really does make waste! First we have to stop and pack a survival kit for the road. We have to fill that kit with basic information about the concepts and terms associated with language and communication. We have to fill it with basic communication techniques and strategies. Starting with . . .

The Four Reasons Why
Good Communication Is So Important

I'm not going to tell you that good communication is important because it's part of being a better person, or part of moving humanity toward moral and intellectual superiority, or anything else of that kind. These statements may be true. Good communication and language skills may be the heart of all ethics and esthetics and philosophy. But I'm not a philosopher, or a theologian, or even an image counselor. I am a practical person who has spent her life dealing with the same problems *you* have to deal with. I'm going to give you four practical down-to-earth reasons why you aren't safe saying, "Oh, it's only talk! We have lots more important things to worry about than *talk!*" If that ever was true, it's true no longer. And here are the reasons why.

✦ REASON ONE: Language and health are tightly linked.

We're used to being told that we can't expect to stay fit and healthy unless we pay close attention to a long list of hazards and risk factors in our lives. Cholesterol. Nicotine. Power tools. Over-weight. Alcohol. Speedometers. Exercise. Germs — our germs and other people's. The list goes on and on. Sometimes it seems as though there's nothing on this earth that isn't a threat. What we *haven't* been told — because until quite recently nobody knew it — is that these hazards aren't the ones we most need to worry about.

As long as researchers were only able to look at the health histories of relatively small groups of people, tracked over only a few years, the items on that list *did* seem to be our main concern. But once we had computers powerful enough to look at health histories of *hundreds of thousands of people over many decades of their lifetimes* — a recent development — we suddenly realized that we'd been missing the most important patterns. The research we're able to do now shows us clearly and dramatically that the real hazards to our health, for all diseases and disorders and accidents across the board, are simply these two: hostility, and loneliness.

You're in far more danger from exposure to hostilty and loneliness than from exposure to the things you're used to worrying about. The more extensive your exposure, the more often it occurs, the longer and more chronic it is, the greater the danger you face. And hostility and loneliness can't be considered separately, because there's no quicker way to become a lonely person than to be a hostile one.

Very few human beings express their hostility by blowing things up and burning things down. Ninety-nine percent of us, whatever our age, express hostility primarily through our *language*. The only way we can reduce the hostility and loneliness that threatens us is by using language that will reduce and defuse hostility in our lives and help us build strong social networks. And nothing we can do to guard the health and fitness of our children is as important as seeing to it that their *language* environment doesn't poison them and make all our other efforts worthless.

You can give a child the very best diet, the finest medical care, the most abundant opportunities for games and sports, all the traditional advantages. But if that child spends his or her young life in an environment where people do nothing but blame and argue and plead and threaten and put one another down from morning till night — or where the most frequent kind of language is silence — you've wasted your time and money and energy. That child will not be healthy, and neither will anybody else who has to live in that environment.

✦ REASON TWO: Verbal violence and physical violence are tightly linked.

I said above that most human beings express hostility primarily through language, and that's accurate. It's a sad comment on our society that a large number of human beings also express hostility with *physical* violence, which is now an epidemic in the United States. However, almost nobody past the age of diapers just walks up to another person and starts hitting. First there are angry words; first there is an argument; only then does the hitting begin.

You may think you can blame your high taxes and high cost of living on politicians and incompetent bureaucracies. You would be wrong. Those things are expensive, but they aren't where most of our money goes. *Most of our money is spent protecting society against physical violence and dealing with its consequences.* Most of our money goes for insurance and law enforcement and metal detectors and judges and prisons and emergency departments and all the rest of the things we have to have to survive the physical violence in this country. If we could get physical violence — which begins, 99 percent of the time, with *verbal* violence — under control, we would have plenty of money for everything else we need. The cure for our raging national debt and deficit isn't a balanced budget amendment, it's language used in such a way that verbal violence is dealt with effectively while it's still verbal, so that it *doesn't* escalate to physical violence.

The cure for violence, and the chance for everyone (not just the very wealthy) to have a comfortable and decent lifestyle, has to begin with the language used in the home. No other solution exists that has even a modest hope of success.

✦ REASON THREE: Good communication skills and success are tightly linked.

There was a time when people could assume that their children — if they finished high school and acquired "work ethic" habits such as showing up on time — would be able to go get a decent job and make a pretty decent living. People knew that youngsters might take a few "trial" jobs in their teens but would soon settle into a field where they could either hang on to their position (and count on a regular package of benefits and a series of raises over time) or advance steadily to a higher position. Job changes would be few, and a career change after thirty would be almost unheard of. Parents could assume that their adult children would work in situations where they were well known and others had time to get to know them and understand their personal foibles and problems. In that world, there was plenty of time to work everything out, there was job security, and all that mattered was the motivation to do a job well.

That world is gone. So far as anyone can tell, it's gone forever. We live in a world now where earning a decent living means being ready to change jobs — and careers — at the drop of a hat, not just once or twice but many times. A world where machines constantly replace human beings by doing the work humans used to do. We've seen whole populations of workers — telephone operators and backup musicians and assembly-line workers and typists — disappear from the workforce, replaced by machines. We live in the world of outsourcing and downsizing, of temporary workers and independent contractors.

It's not enough today to be willing and able to work hard; it's not enough to have one set of well-honed skills. Today's successful adult must have the ability to move into a group of total strangers and quickly establish good relationships with them that will last as long as the job (or the job training) does. And this must be done over and over again, with new groups, until retirement.

The one crucial factor for doing that is good communication skills. And that one factor is rapidly dividing our population into two groups: the Haves, who can expect roughly the sorts of opportunities their parents had; and the Have-Nots, who can expect only low-wage and low-status jobs for their entire working lives, followed by retirement into poverty. There's no middle ground any more, and language skills determine which of the two extremes children will fall into as adults.

It's nice to be able to give your children training in tennis and golf and ballet and piano and figure skating. These skills can be a big help in adult life. But *nothing* will help kids as much, and go as far toward making them successful and independent adults, as good language skills. And nobody but parents and primary caregivers can provide *that* training during the formative years when children are best equipped to learn language skills.

The teachers in our schools don't have time to do this. They have to deal with thirty or more children at once, many of whom have special needs (including the inability to speak the teacher's language). The television set — which demonstrates that the person with the meanest mouth always gets the biggest laughs, and where "talk" shows are not talk but no-holds-barred verbal slugfests — is not going to provide that training. Certainly other *children* can't be expected to do the job! It has be done by the only people who have years of one-on-one time with the children — the people, usually parents, they live with. Your time with your kids may be limited, but you have more of it than anyone else does, and it's a precious resource that you *cannot* afford to waste.

✦ REASON FOUR: Communication skills are your family inheritance.

You may not be able to leave your children a large fortune; most of us can't. We do the best we can, and often our best doesn't include mansions and yachts. But there's one legacy that all parents do leave to their kids, whether they want to or not: *the family communication strategies.*

If your children are past the toddler stage, you may be prepared to tell me that they'd rather be drawn and quartered than use the language they hear *you* use. They don't want to talk the way you talk. They think your vocabulary and your conversational style are stuffy or nerdy or worse. I understand that, and I think it's true a great deal of the time, especially for adolescent children. But what the kids are rejecting is the parts of your language behavior they're *consciously* aware of — and that's a long way from being all there is.

Behind and/or beneath such matters as your word choices and the rules you follow to put your sentences together, there's a whole lot more to your grammar, including the *strategies* you use when you communicate. Strategies for heading off arguments or for provoking them. Strategies for convincing others to do what you want them to do and persuading them not to do things you're opposed to. Strategies for circling the truth when you don't want to tell it and finding out if others are doing that to *you*. Strategies for negotiating agreements. Strategies for rewarding and punishing. Your children may use different words and slang and different styles, but unless something unusual happens in their lives they will use the communication strategies they learned from observing *you*.

When the strategies you model for your children are good ones, it will mean more to them and do more for them than any other inheritance can, in the long run. If, on the other hand, the strategies you show them are the kind that turn a home into a combat zone or a misery zone, they'll inherit that from you, too — and they will probably go on and hand it on down to your grandchildren. You can write a will to keep your kids from inheriting money you think would be put to better use somewhere else. But there's not one thing you can do to set aside your communication strategies so that your children won't carry them on into adult life. That will happen, and it gives new meaning to the field of estate planning.

These four basic units of information about the importance of communication work together: Whatever you do about any one of them will have consequences for the other three. That makes things easier.

Now, we can move on to . . .

The Seven Most Important Principles for Language between Adults and Youngsters

✦ PRINCIPLE ONE: Every human language is a rule-governed *system*.

The way people usually talk and write about language makes it obvious that they aren't really aware of this principle. Fully competent adults, educated and sophisticated and successful, will look me right in the eye and say, "You know, I don't really know anything about grammar; I never did well in it at school and I took as few grammar classes as I possibly could." A survey in *USA Today* for November 18, 1994, reported that although 78 percent of teachers want parents to help their kids with their writing, only 16 percent of parents felt that they *knew* enough to be any use to the children.

This is ridiculous. If people really didn't "know anything about grammar," meaning that they just used words and body language at random, they'd say one of an infinite number of possible strings of gibberish like this one:

> "Know you, I not know really about grammar nothing; never did I in it school at well, took as few I grammar classes as could I possibly and."

That just plain does not happen. *Ever.* Not in the language of adults, and not in the language of children.

✦ PRINCIPLE TWO: Every normal human being has a complete and flawless grammar of his or her native language stored in long-term memory.

Please put this principle into your memory right now, and remember it forever!

Our internal grammars aren't identical. When people speak different dialects of a single language, the rules their grammars contain are largely the same, but not *exactly* the same. (That's how we *know* they're dialects of a single language.)

My own grammar has a rule that I follow by saying, "You'll need yourall's umbrellas — it's raining outside!" For me, "your umbrellas" refers only to one person's two or more umbrellas. Your grammar almost certainly does *not* have that rule. But I don't talk randomly, nor do you, and we're all following the rules of our native grammars. Except when there is severe mental retardation or a medical catastrophe, that second principle applies to *everybody*. And, most importantly for communication across the generation gap, *it's true by about the age of five or six.* (I know this is the age at which we feel obligated to start "teaching" children their grammar; nevertheless, it's true.)

◆ PRINCIPLE THREE: Children are born with the ability to learn the grammar of their language just by observing the language others use in their environment.

Children don't learn languages the way pigeons learn to peck at a bar to get a piece of corn. At birth their brains already contain the complete set of possible specifications for a human language. What the kids do is learn which of those specifications apply in *their* language, by observing the language used around them. They're not born already knowing a language. If they don't see and hear language during this critical period they'll never be able to use it normally. Giving them a cookie when they say something that sounds a little like "cookie" to you will encourage them to say it again, and they'll learn to be careful about saying things that get them punished. The input they get from others who already speak a language is very important, because it's their *model.* But they don't learn languages the way adults have to learn them — painfully, by memorizing rules and patterns that have to be constantly rehearsed and struggled with. Children's brains have language-learning equipment that adult brains don't have. That's why we so often see immigrant families in which, although the whole family has heard English for the same number of years, only the children speak it without a foreign accent.

◆ PRINCIPLE FOUR: The only meaning a sequence of language has in the real world is the meaning the *listener* understands it to have.

Once upon a time, communication was thought to be the linguistic equivalent of the United Parcel Service (UPS). When I put a hat into a package and send it to someone, I take it for granted that the person it goes to will find a hat inside when the package is opened. When I was a schoolchild I was taught that communication worked roughly the same way: *If I had a thought, and I chose my words carefully when I spoke that thought aloud, the person listening to me would find that same thought in his or her head.* But that's not true. If UPS worked the way communication works, I'd have no reason to be surprised when the box I put a hat into was opened by someone else and what the person found inside was a pair of shoes.

You can have the best intentions in the world when you talk to others. You can mull over your thought until it's absolutely clear to you and choose your words with exquisite care. But the only meaning your listeners will use as a basis for action and *re*action is the meaning *they* give your words, and it may be quite a bit different from the meaning you intended. This is even more true when you talk to children, because their *experience* with communication is so much more limited than yours is.

✦ PRINCIPLE FIVE: All communication is an interactive feedback loop, and any loop you *feed* will grow.

Except when language has been memorized (in a play, for example), we all base what we say on what was said to us. The people who hear us talk base what they say back on what they heard us say to them, and so on around and around the loop. Even the very first line we say in a conversation is usually based at least in part on something another person said at an earlier time.

If I think that you dislike me — because of something I heard you (or someone else) say yesterday — my first sentence in a conversation with you will be affected by that. My attitude toward you won't be neutral and open, and I'll be expecting something negative from you. You'll sense that as I talk, and you're likely to react to it by saying something that has just a touch of hostility or reserve. This will make me believe I was *right* about your bad feeling toward me, and that will be reflected in the *next* thing I say. We have to be careful about the kinds of loops we set up and feed, and this is just as true when talking with children as it is when we talk with adults.

✦ PRINCIPLE SIX: Talking to a child, especially after the age of five or six, is essentially the same thing as talking to an adult you outrank.

This principle is often hard for people to believe. Because children's vocabularies are smaller, because they sometimes say "wabbit" for "rabbit," because their experience of the world is limited, we tend to feel that there must be some special way of talking to a child of six and another way of talking to a child of nine and yet another special way to talk to a teenager. That's not how it works.

Once a child knows the basic grammar of the language, by about the age of five or six, talking to children should be no different from talking to adults who are our subordinates (that is, adults we're allowed to give orders to). This means that — within reason — we should listen to children with the same attention as when we listen to adults. It means we should be no more likely to interrupt a child than to interrupt an adult; we should give children in conversation the same benefit of the doubt we give adults. It doesn't mean that we should spoil children or let them say any old thing they want to say, or that we should let them dominate our conversations and make adult conversations impossible. It *does* mean that many adults need to make some changes in the way they communicate with children.

✦ PRINCIPLE SEVEN: Most communication problems are in the language, not in the person.

When we don't like what we hear someone say, we have a tendency to leap to conclusions about the person who's talking. We decide that the words were said because "He's mean" or "She's prejudiced against me" or "He doesn't like short people" or "She thinks I'm boring." When we talk to children, our conclusions may be even worse. We may decide that the kids are being insolent or defiant, we may decide that they're showing off or trying to provoke us, when the real problem is that they're just inexperienced in carrying on conversations with adults. We need to change that tendency and lean hard the other way.

Like the four reasons why communication is so important, these seven basic principles all work together, interdependently and synergistically. This means that anything you do with regard to one will have consequences for all the others. And it goes without saying: You can't separate these two sets of information either. That is a *characteristic* of systems (as opposed to something random).

Now, with this information in our road survival kit, we're ready to start moving toward the on ramps and out into the traffic with the children.

◆

CHAPTER 1

We're not fighting — we're just talking!

Using the Language Traffic Rules

────── Scenario One ──────

Joan was too angry to eat; she put her fork down and stopped trying. "Now, look here!" she said. "I want to spend my vacation with my family!"

"Fine!" Grant answered, keeping his eyes on his steak. "Then we agree on that."

"No, we don't agree!"

"What I think," twelve-year-old Amy began. . . . But her mother went right on talking, drowning her out, and Amy had to settle for an outraged "HONestly! You'd think I was the invisible PERson or something!"

"You know very well what I mean, Grant Hinton!" Joan insisted. "I am sick of sitting around for a whole week every year listening to you and your brother and his wife talk about football! This year, I want to _____"

"I know what you want to do, honey," said Grant. "You want to shop. For a week. Why don't you just set up a tent in the mall?"

Across the table, sixteen-year-old Jason snickered, groaned loudly, and laid his head down on his arms in mock despair. "Way to go, Dad," he said sarcastically. "Let's go straight for the jugular, as long as we're here! Nothing like a pleasant family dinner, I always say!"

"Mother!" Amy protested, her voice getting higher and whinier with every word, "LOOK at him! He's got his FACE right in his PLATE! Eeeuuh! How am I supposed to EAT with _____"

"Will you kids PLEASE keep quiet?" Grant broke in. "Your mother and I are TRYING TO TALK!"

"Grant! Please!" said Joan. "You could at least TRY to control yourself! Everybody on the block can hear you YELLing!"

"I am NOT yelling!"

"Well, it sure sounds like yelling to ME!"

"Grant," said Joan, her voice shaking but determined, "can't we at least talk about this reasonably?"

"I'm talking reasonably."

"You're not! Your mind is completely closed. You're just _____"

"Joan," he said, through gritted teeth, "if you want to go someplace else, you go right ahead. But the kids and I are going to the river!"

"I'd rather go to the mall," Jason observed.

"HEY!" Grant jabbed at the air in Jason's direction with his fork. "YOU had better watch your MOUTH, buddy!"

"Well, come on, Dad, YOU were the one that said _____"

"How come HE gets to talk again?" Amy shrieked. "How come NObody ever listens to MEEeee??"

———————————— ✦ ————————————

What's Going On Here?

This is, I'm sorry to say, typical of what passes for family communication in many homes. The Hintons are actually fond of one another. Joan and Grant would tell you that they have a good marriage and that they love their kids very much. A friend or relative who came in in the middle of Scenario One and was concerned would be assured that all was well. "We're not fighting," the Hintons would say. "We're just talking."

If this happened *only* when there was a disagreement about something important, that would be one thing. But the Hintons' mealtime conversation is like this *every* night. Joan and Grant talk about whatever interests them, interrupting and contradicting each other freely. When they disagree, they're not shy about showing it; they use very harsh language. Jason and Amy are shut out of their parents' dialogue, but they keep trying to break in. The linguistic crowbar Jason relies on is the Smart Crack, learned from sixteen

years of observing his parents and the television set. Amy is out-
classed right now by the older speakers, so she falls back on whining, wailing, and shrieking.

Here's an example of the Hintons' dinner conversation when
they have nothing important to argue about:

Joan: "Do you like the pecans in that chicken, Grant?"

Amy: "Well, I don't! I think they're _____ "

Jason: "Nobody asked you, Shorty!"

Grant: "Jason, don't be so rude to your sister!"

Jason: "Well, she interrupted! You call that polite?"

Grant: "Joan, what were you asking me?"

Joan: "I don't remember."

Amy   "You wanted to know if he likes all those yucky nuts in
the chicken!"

Jason: "Hey . . . listen to the Gobbling GourMET, will you?"

Amy: "YOU think you're SMART, DON'T you! JUST because
YOU _____ "

Grant: "I don't know, honey. Maybe pecans are a little bit over-
powering for chicken. Maybe if you _____ "

Joan: "You know, I'll bet walnuts would be better."

In both examples, even when the only argument going on is the
kids' ritual exchange of insults, dinner at the Hintons is more like a
traffic jam at a crowded intersection than a pleasant family gather-
ing. And the body language that goes with the words is made up of
one unpleasant item after another, with Jason's face-in-his-plate tactics taking the top honors.

It's easy to laugh about this. Certainly audiences laugh at the
television sitcoms that feature this same brand of table talk. It's easy
to say "Oh, well—that's just the way they talk! What difference
does it make, as long they love each other?"

The answer to that question is: It makes a *lot* of difference! For Joan and Grant, these language patterns guarantee that when they have several messages to communicate over dinner they'll be lucky to get even one across. And in the confusion, even that one message is likely to be misunderstood — leading to dialogues like this:

Joan: "But I thought you said you didn't <u>like</u> the pecans!"

Grant: "I never said that."

Joan: "I'm <u>sure</u> you did! Last night at dinner."

Grant: "No. What I <u>said</u> was _____ "

For Jason and Amy, there's little chance that any message of theirs will be part of the conversation unless it represents an emergency. The model of human conversation the children watch each evening is badly flawed, and they get no chance to observe (or participate in) anything better. Like most busy modern families, these four people have few chances to sit down together and talk. If either Jason or Amy has a problem that ought to be discussed *before* it becomes an emergency, the dinner table is likely to be the only opportunity. As that opportunity is wasted, night after night, year after year, the chances keep growing that Joan and Grant will find themselves facing a grave — or even tragic — situation and saying, "But the child never said a <u>word</u>! We had <u>no</u> <u>idea</u> there was anything wrong!"

Finally, the frantic atmosphere at the table — with everybody struggling to grab some small piece of attention and constantly being frustrated in that struggle — is unhealthy for the Hintons. It's bad for their hearts and their blood pressures and their digestive systems, and it's bad for their emotional balance. Human beings aren't designed for constant unrelenting competition; under that kind of stress and strain, they wear out fast.

Dr. Benjamin Spock says that the one thing he'd most like to tell the parents who are his readers is this:

> That young children are watching them all the time and patterning themselves after their parents. . . . They should realize that all children are trying very hard to be as much like their parents as they can be.
>
> (Interview, 1992)

Deborah Franklin (in "Charm School for Bullies," *Hippocrates,* May–June 1989) reports on extensive research into the *future* behavior of children who act like Jason and Amy. It shows that "those who bullied in elementary school—acted rudely to the teacher and other children, started fights over nothing, took classmates' toys without asking—were five times more likely than their less belligerent classmates to have been convicted of crimes by age 30." When these children grew up they were far more likely to be working in low-paying jobs, to be guilty of spouse abuse, and "to be raising contentious children of their own." We're getting a clear message today both from research and from our common sense that "Hey, this is just the way we talk!" isn't good enough. We have to do better than that.

What to Do About It—
Using the Language Traffic Rules

The Hintons' situation isn't hopeless. They're not cruel people who get a kick out of hurting one another. There are lots of simple things they could do to improve their family communication dramatically. Their first step should be to start following the *language traffic rules*.

Language Is Traffic

Metaphors (like "Time is money" or "War is hell") are our most powerful linguistic tool for changing attitudes quickly—and with a good chance that the change will last. Unlike what happens with punishments or rewards, which may change behavior but rarely change the feelings that lie *behind* behavior, people who are persuaded by a metaphor *feel* differently about the situation. When you're dealing with children, especially older ones, persuasion by metaphor is always best. Kids who do something *only* because they know they'll be punished if they refuse will do it as slowly and as badly as they dare. Things they do only for a reward don't carry this built-in sabotage factor, but motivation for a reward is temporary. When children do something because your language has persuaded them that they *want* to do it, or (if it's something undesirable) that they *should* do it, the results will be far better, and you'll have set a good precedent. Metaphors are your best strategy for persuading with language.

I used to feel insulted when people around me left their television sets on while we talked. That seemed to me to mean they were wishing I'd leave so they could watch TV. But when I read Camille Paglia's explanation (in the March 1992 issue of *Harper's*) that for her generation the TV set is the flickering fire on the hearth, my feelings changed — instantly and completely. The TV still bothers me when people leave it on during conversation, but I don't feel *insulted* about it any longer. I wouldn't feel insulted if my hosts left a fire burning in their fireplace while we talked; why, then, would I find it rude for them to leave a television set playing softly? *Only metaphors have the power to work this kind of transformation. Punishments, rewards, and logic don't even come close.*

One reason metaphors work so fast is that they're a lot like holograms: one small piece is enough to evoke the whole. When everybody in a group is familiar with the metaphor — the way most Americans are familiar with the metaphors of *The Football Game* and *The Old West* — communication is easy and efficient. A few words, like "I'm counting on you to carry the ball for us" or "Wagons, ho!," will bring the metaphor to everybody's minds, and people will fill in the details for themselves automatically.

We can therefore call on the metaphor "Language is traffic" to accomplish two valuable tasks. First: to make clear how conversation *ought* to be carried on, no matter what the speakers' ages. And second: to lay down a foundation from which to work out the details when we're faced with new communication situations. Almost everybody in our society drives a car; almost everybody who doesn't drive spends much time in traffic, as a passenger. Even very small children play with tiny cars and ride around in larger ones. A traffic metaphor will be understood immediately by anyone five or older, and much of it will be clear even to toddlers. Let's look at it.

Road Traffic

1. Road traffic exists to move people and goods around.

2. Unless it's done right, the people and goods won't reach their destinations or will arrive damaged.

3. Because trucks and cars are powerful and potentially dangerous, and because every driver is equipped with one, we know we all have to agree on a set of rules so that it *can* be done right — especially for getting on and off the road and making it safely through intersections.

Language Traffic

1. Language traffic exists to move information — *messages with meaningful content* — around.

2. Unless it's done right, the messages won't reach their destinations or will arrive damaged.

3. While a speeding smart crack may not seem as immediately powerful and dangerous as a speeding truck, we have good evidence that language can do just as much damage as a collision can. And because every person in a language interaction is equipped with his or her own personal grammar and vocabulary for moving messages around, we know we all have to agree on a set of language traffic rules — especially for getting on and off the conversational floor and making it safely through linguistic intersections.

Road Hogs and Floor Hogs

When you look at the descriptions of the two kinds of traffic, you see right away that they're just two versions of the same thing. But many intelligent and competent people who would never think of breaking the traffic rules on the road regularly ignore the *language* traffic rules. They're disgusted by road hogs, but they routinely hog the conversational floor. They're outraged by speeders and drivers who wander out of their lanes, but in conversation they act as if none of the rules apply to them. Once in a while this is because they're just rude people with no consideration for others, sure. But *most* of the time the problem isn't malice, it's a lack of information. People obey the rules of the road because they understand the system and want it to work properly. Where language traffic is concerned, though, either they don't know what the rules *are*, or they don't know why the rules should apply to them. *They don't under-stand the system formed* by the rules.

Let's clear this up. We'll start with the pattern for a hypothetical perfect conversation among adults and compare it with a perfect experience on the road. This pattern is the *model* that parents and other adults need to present to children, so that the kids will have a chance to observe it in action. Then we'll come back to the special difficulties of conversation between adults and children. Let's assume that three adults, Tom, Frank, and Ann, are the speakers in our example.

The Traffic Pattern

1. Ann introduces a topic that is neither boring nor offensive to Tom and Frank, and talks about it for no more than three sentences of reasonable length.

   Get out on the road in a car or truck that underlines *works, and move right along at the normal speed.*

2. While Ann is talking, both Tom and Frank listen, without inter-rupting.

   Stay in your own lane, and wait for your turn at the intersections.

3. When Ann is near the end of her turn to talk, she signals that to Frank and Tom, and Frank signals that he wants to talk next. Ann closes her turn by slowing down, ending her sentence, and pausing. Then she hands the turn to Frank by eye contact or by speaking to him directly.

   When you're going to slow down or stop or turn, signal your intention to the people sharing the road with you. If another dri-ver signals an intention to move into a lane or make a turn, wait until that's finished before you go on. When you *want to turn or merge, be sure that other people around you know that and are safely out of the way before you go ahead.*

4. Frank takes up Ann's topic and supports it, for no more than three sentences, while Ann and Tom listen; he does not change

the subject. Then, since Tom hasn't talked yet, Frank makes eye contact with him to indicate that he's willing to give him the next turn. If Tom doesn't *accept* the turn, Frank gives it back to Ann.

This goes on until (a) everybody has had a chance to say a few sentences on Ann's topic (or has been offered that chance and turned it down), and (b) all messages needed for the conversation have been transmitted. If anybody seems to need help moving things along, the others do what they can to provide it.

Take turns going through the intersections or getting into the lanes until everybody makes it. If somebody is having trouble getting into a lane or through a turn, do what you can to help.

5. One of the three speakers introduces a *new* topic and steps 1–4 are repeated — or the conversation ends.

   When you get to your destination, either choose another one and head for it or get your car off the road.

6. Emergency Option: When there's a valid reason not to follow the pattern, the person who breaks the rules explains why it's necessary, as politely as possible.

   If you're driving a fire truck to a fire, or an ambulance to an accident scene, turn on your siren and your lights — and don't drive faster than you <u>have</u> to.

We could draw many more parallels here between these two kinds of traffic. But you'll notice that we don't need to. Because this is a metaphor, and because you know both parts of it well, you have no trouble drawing them yourself.

It's important not to dismiss this pattern as "only being polite." Sure it's polite to follow the guidelines — but that's not why most people do it. We follow the rules of road traffic because it's not *safe* to ignore them; we should follow the language traffic rules for exactly the same reason.

Most children aren't very concerned about "manners." Teenagers often actively work to *avoid* being polite; that's part of their adolescent rebellion. Telling youngsters to follow the rules of language traffic "because it's polite" or claiming that that's why *you* do it won't impress them nearly as much as "because it's dangerous not to." Use the power of the traffic metaphor to help you get through the linguistic barriers youngsters like to raise, quickly and efficiently.

Following the Language Traffic Rules in Adult–Child Conversations

The use of the language traffic system in conversations between adults and youngsters has two parts:

1. Modeling conversations for children to observe.

2. Carrying on conversations with children.

Modeling Conversations for Children

This is the easy part. You decide that you'll do it and you follow through. Ask yourself: If the kids around you don't learn conversational skills from you, where *will* they learn them? Not in school, that's for sure; schools don't have conversation classes. Not from television. The language behavior on television sitcoms and game shows and so-called talk shows is rarely good conversation; much of the time it's conversation-as-combat. If your conversations in front of children in the past have been like those between Grant and Joan in Scenario One, you'll realize now that you've been training the kids to follow that example. To fix that, you need to begin following the language traffic rules yourself. There are three possibilities, when you do:

1. The people you usually talk to in front of children already follow the language traffic rules; all you have to do is join them.

2. The people you usually talk to in front of children can be *persuaded* to join you in following the language traffic rules, either because they're naturally cooperative or because you're able to

convince them to be. (I suggest using the language traffic metaphor — plus the fact that adults are the models for children's language behavior — as your tools for persuasion.)

3. The people you usually talk to in front of children absolutely will not follow the language traffic rules, no matter what you say to them. In that case, you need to do two things:

    First: Demonstrate for the kids how adults deal with people like that. (Later chapters in this book will help you with this.)

    Second: Recruit some other, more cooperative, adults to serve as models.

Carrying On Conversations with Children

This is the hard part! You have to let a child choose and introduce the conversational topic. You have to support that topic through a few conversational turns, instead of switching to a topic of your own choice. You have to give the floor back to the child every few sentences. And — hardest of all — you have to *listen* while the child talks, with your full and courteous attention. Even when you're the one who starts the conversation, so that you get to choose the topic, you still have to rely on the child to support it, and everything else stays the same, including the listening.

If your first reaction is that children can't *do* this, because they don't know the traffic rules and therefore can't apply them, you've made my point for me. You're right — *unless* they've had plenty of chances to observe other people following those rules in their language environment. But stop and think. Suppose you're a good tennis player and you want the children you're fond of to learn to play tennis with you. You'd expect that they wouldn't know the rules of tennis; you'd expect them to make a lot of mistakes at first and need lots of help and patience from you. *That wouldn't strike you as a reason not to teach them tennis.* Teaching them to carry on a conversation with you is exactly the same thing.

Let's look at the two most common problems that come up in adult–child conversations and talk about how to manage them. (We will assume, of course, that you — the adult — *are* following the rules in these language interactions with the child.)

When the Child Ignores the Turn-Taking Rules

What if you're talking with a six-year-old boy and he not only interrupts you but launches into monologues that go on and on forever every time you let him have a turn?

You'll be tempted either to break off the conversation — which won't teach the child anything useful — or to teach by abrupt and explicit instruction. As in, "Stop interrupting me! And when you get a turn to talk, don't run it into the ground!" Or "Nobody's ever going to want to talk to you if you keep hogging the floor and interrupting all the time!" There are times when messages like that are necessary. But it's much better to deal with this problem by *discussing* it with the child and using metaphor power instead of brute verbal force. Look at the following dialogue, in which a father tries to help one of these floor-hogging children. You'll notice that, to accomplish this goal, he has to do some interrupting himself.

DIALOGUE 1

Father: "Johnny, suppose you want to drive to the game and you have to get through that intersection by the fire station. What do you think would happen if you just cut in front of everybody and drove on through it without waiting for the green light?"

Son: "I'd have a wreck! And _____"

Father: "Right! And what if you pulled out in the middle of the intersection and just sat there . . . maybe eating your lunch . . . while everybody else waited?"

Son: "Boy, that would be dumb! And _____"

Father: "Well, suppose you did that. Do you think other people would want you on the road?"

Son: "Nah . . . they'd take away my license, I bet. And _____"

Father: "<u>Right.</u> So maybe you ought to think about how people feel when they try to <u>talk</u> with you and you keep cutting them off and not letting anybody else get a word in edgewise. What do you think?"

It's important, once the point has been made, for this grownup to give the turn back to the child and follow the rules from then on. *Lecturing isn't conversation, either.* If every conversation a child has with you turns into a lecture, the child will learn only one thing: to do everything possible to avoid talking with you.

Don't be a fanatic about the pattern for a perfect conversation, by the way. It's just a goal to keep in mind and work toward. Most adult conversations *aren't* perfect. Adults interrupt each other, or talk at the same time, or overlap the ends of one another's sentences. Adults sometimes go on talking for more than three sentences, and sometimes their sentences are too long. Ideally, they do this because they know when it's *okay* to bend or break the rules. That is, they not only know the rules, they know the *meta*rules — like the rule for choosing one rule instead of another one. As long as youngsters watching them can see that they're *trying* for good conversation, not just out there on the language highway trying to stop traffic and cause wrecks, it will be all right.

In the same way that in real traffic — either on the highway or in conversational space — adults cut each other a little slack, they should be reasonable in conversation with children. When the kids go too far, help them become aware of that, just as you would if you were a passenger in a car they were driving and they went too far in taking liberties with the rules of the road.

When You Have to Listen to the Child

Now we come to the problem of *listening* to children. Often this is anything but easy. Children often choose topics that are excruciatingly boring to adults, like "my teddy" or "why I hate green beans." Or they choose topics that turn an adult's stomach. Like the child in the next dialogue:

DIALOGUE 2

Adult: "Well . . . what did you do at school today?"

Child: "It was really neat."

Adult: "Oh? What happened?"

Child: "You know Billy Everett? Well, right after we said the Pledge Allegiance he threw up, right on the floor by his desk. And it was all red and gooshy and _____"

Adult: "Hey! That's enough! Go put your backpack away and get ready to do your homework!"

It's reasonable for this child to go off thinking, "If you didn't want me to tell you what happened at school, why did you ask me?" You can't assume that the child will know why the adult has violated the traffic rules and cut off the conversation this way. How would the child know? What if the conversation went this way:

DIALOGUE 2 REVISITED

Adult: "Well . . . what did you do at school today?"

Child: "It was really neat."

Adult: "Oh? What happened?"

Child: "You know Billy Everett? Well, right after we said the Pledge of Allegiance, he threw up, right on the floor by his desk. And it was all red and gooshy and _____"

Adult: "Wait, honey — stop. You need to know something. If you try to talk to people about how it looked when somebody threw up, they won't listen to you, and they'll probably get mad."

Child: "Why? It was neat!"

Adult: "Because it makes them feel sick at their stomachs to hear you talk about it."

Child: "That's weird!"

Adult: "I give you my word—that's the way it is. Try to remember that. Okay?"

Child: "Don't talk about throw-up."

Adult: "Right. Exactly right! Now—what <u>else</u> happened at school today?"

This is an example of a situation where adults *should* offer direct and specific instruction. Nothing in a child's brain is going to provide a list of what things adults find offensive—that has to be taught. Do it as quickly as possible, and without shaming the child, whether the problem is a disgusting topic or a four-letter word the child has heard somewhere and is trying out on you. Let the child know that when they say those things people will get angry. And once you've made your point (and at the same time demonstrated how this kind of interrupting is done) your next move is to let the child go on and finish the interrupted turn.

Children also are likely to say things that adults find not just boring or offensive but just plain *ridiculous*. It may be very important to listen to them carefully anyway. For example, look at the following dialogue, between a mother and a five-year-old child.

DIALOGUE 3

Child: "Mama, do I <u>have</u> to go to school today? I don't <u>want</u> to!"

Mother: "Of <u>course</u> you have to go to school."

Child: "But I don't <u>want</u> to! I'm <u>scared</u>!"

Mother: "Scared of what? Tell me quick, now—I'm busy!"

Child: "There's gonna be <u>lep</u>rechauns!"

Mother: "Oh, for heaven's <u>sakes</u>! You go get ready for school this <u>min</u>ute, and let me get my <u>work</u> done!"

No adult would deal with another adult's fear this way. But this is an example of a common problem in adult–child communication. This adult, because she's busy, isn't willing to listen to the child.

When a quick question doesn't get an answer that meets her specifications for "something important enough to give my attention to," the adult pulls rank and runs the child right off the conversational road.

Psychologist George Miller once said something so important to human communication that I call it *Miller's Law*. He said:

> In order to understand what another person is saying, you must assume that it is true and try to imagine what it could be true of.
> (Interview with Elizabeth Hall, 1980)

Unfortunately, our tendency (especially when we're busy or distracted) is to use what we might call *Miller's-Law-in-Reverse*. That is: When we hear something that strikes us negatively, we assume that it's *false*, and we try to imagine what could be wrong with the person who said it. We do that even with other adults; children, low as they are on the pecking order, have little defense against the practice. The parent in this dialogue has decided—on the basis of almost no evidence—that naughtiness is the reason for the child's utterance.

When adults listen to children, they need to make a real effort to apply Miller's Law. Other adults may be willing to keep trying to get a message across after they're rejected on the first attempt, but children often don't have enough self-confidence to do that. We need to remember that kids don't have nearly as much information about what's unreasonable, unlikely, or impossible as adults do; we have to make allowances for that.

Suppose the parent in the dialogue had followed Miller's Law with her child. How might that dialogue have turned out? Look at another version of Dialogue 3:

DIALOGUE 3 REVISITED

Child: "Mama, do I <u>have</u> to go to school today? I don't <u>want</u> to!"

Mother: "Of <u>course</u> you have to go to school."

Child: "But I don't <u>want</u> to! I'm <u>scared</u>!"

Mother: "Scared of what? Tell me quick, now—I'm busy."

Child: "There's gonna be le_p_rechauns!"

Mother: "Leprechauns . . . Oh, right — it's Saint Patrick's Day. But I don't understand. Why are you afraid of leprechauns?"

Child: "Mama, they jump on people out of the trees, and they eat them!"

Mother: "Oh! I know what the problem is! Honey — it's leopards that do that, not le_p_rechauns. The words sound alike, I know, but they're not the same thing at all. A leprechaun is absolutely safe. I promise."

Adults who hear something from a child that makes them think, "Oh, for heaven sakes! I don't have time for that kind of nonsense!" only need to take time to do the kind of quick investigation shown in the revised dialogue. You want to know, after assuming that what the child has said is true, what it could be true of. For example, "It's dangerous for me to go to school on St. Patrick's Day" would be true of a world where "leprechaun" means the same thing as "leopard." Adults have more than enough information to figure things like this out; they just have to stop and ask a quick question or two, starting with, "I don't understand," to encourage the child to explain. (My thanks to Rebecca Haden for the leprechaun/leopard example.)

Children who seem to you to waste your time in ridiculous conversations are exactly like the kids who, when trying to play tennis or checkers with you, bore you by keeping you waiting while they try to figure out what to do next, or annoy you by hitting the tennis ball wildly out of bounds or jumping your checkers when they're not allowed to. *They have to learn.* And conversation, unlike tennis or checkers, is a skill they *must* have if they're going to succeed in adult life.

I understand why so many adults tune children out. I understand why they assume that nothing kids have to say could possibly be worth hearing, or that anything kids say will be infuriating, or both. When adults are very busy or very tired — pretty much the usual situation today — the temptation to do this is almost irresistible. But children who are treated this way will learn *not* to carry on conversations with adults. And then later, when the adults desperately want to talk something over with the child, it won't be possible.

Now let's go back to Scenario One and see how following the language traffic rules might have turned the communication at the Hintons' dinner table into conversation instead of chaos.

Another Look at Scenario One

The first traffic violation in Scenario One happens when Amy tries to join the discussion about where the family should spend its vacation. She only gets as far as "What I think" before her mother cuts her off. Joan Hinton is deeply involved in an argument with her husband, so there's no reason why she should feel willing to set that aside to listen to Amy. But if she wants her daughter to know how to participate in conversation, she has only three choices.

1.   She can ask Amy (politely) to wait briefly for her turn.

> **Amy:** "What I think _____"
>
> **Joan:** "Amy, your opinion is important to me and I want to hear it. If you'll wait just a minute and let me finish what I was about to say, I'll come right back to you."

(And Joan has to follow *through* on that, just as she would with an adult.)

2.   She can listen to Amy, as long as the child follows the language traffic rules.

> **Amy:** "What I think is, we ought to go to the Grand Canyon. That's where Jennifer always goes."
>
> **Joan:** "That might be a good idea, Amy. I went to the Grand Canyon when I was about your age, and I still remember what a good time I had." (*Then she turns to look at Amy's father and speaks to him.*) "Now, Grant, I want you to know that I don't agree with you. I am sick of sitting around for a whole week every year." (Etc.)

(And Joan must be sure that she doesn't rush the interaction with

Amy so much, or switch her attention back to Grant so abruptly, that the child feels she's only being humored. The difference is a matter of five or six seconds; there's time to do it right.)

3. She can listen to Amy, but stop her when it becomes clear that the child plans to do a monologue.

For this third choice, the fact that the interaction between Joan and Grant is an argument makes a difference. In an ordinary conversation Joan should stop and help Amy understand what she's doing wrong. But in the heat of an adult argument that's not realistic, and it's not good for children to get the idea that they have the power to put an adult disagreement on hold that way. In that situation Joan should go straight to the Emergency Option and say, "Amy, this isn't a good time for you to tell us about all the things your friend saw when she went to the Grand Canyon. Daddy and I have to settle this and make a decision now, and you'll have to tell me about Jennifer another time." And then she should turn firmly away from Amy and go on with the conversation.

There are extremes in situations like these. For instance, it's a very bad idea to let children dominate the conversational space and consistently break the language traffic rules. You wouldn't let kids step out into an intersection and direct traffic on the road; you shouldn't allow that in language traffic either. Not only does it keep the adults from being able to carry on a conversation of their own, it also trains children to be people that everybody will try to avoid talking to — both as children and when they grow up. On the other hand, the child whose every attempt to enter a serious adult conversation is met with "Not now, dear; we'll talk about that later!" will stop trying, with the obvious negative consequences. There's a middle ground, and that's what we want to strive for.

Whenever Jason or Amy try to interrupt and join the conversation, the adult Hintons should choose one of the three options above. If the kids are allowed to participate, they won't spend their time talking to each other while their parents are also talking. If this isn't possible — because the conversation between Joan and Grant is restricted to them and the children *can't* participate — then it's a private discussion and shouldn't be going on in front of the kids anyway. When an adults-only topic has to be taken up with children present as a silent audience because it's a genuine emergency, that's fine. When the driver in front of you suddenly pulls off the road because a tire explodes, that's perfectly all right. *Emergencies happen, and exceptions have to be made for them.* But the rest of the time, following the language traffic rules is well worth the effort and will pay it back many times over.

"What We Do at OUR House Is _____"

One last thing should be mentioned here, and that's the issue of *family* rules. Within reason, family rules should take precedence inside the home. What if your family has a rule that says children are not allowed to speak at the table except when an adult speaks to them first? That was the rule at my house when I was a child, and there are still many families where this is the standard. But if you use that rule, remember that the kids will miss the chance to learn from joining in your conversations. You should then follow these guidelines:

- Make sure the conversations when the children are present but not allowed to talk are carried on in a way that makes them good models for the youngsters to observe and learn from.

- Make sure the children get opportunities for adult–child conversations in *other* situations, to make up for the opportunities lost at the table.

When a driver's goal isn't to move people and things from one place to another place but to scare other people off the road, that driver is outside the system and has to be dealt with like anyone else who behaves abnormally. In the same way, a speaker whose goal isn't to keep information moving but to carry out some separate agenda is outside the system. Youngsters observing that speaker won't be learning how to carry on normal conversation. Adults who use their limited conversational space and time with children to reach private goals — like settling a score with another adult or closing a business deal or carrying on a romance — would be wise to keep this in mind and consider doing some rescheduling.

Talking to the Cyberchild

The traffic rules are one area of cross-generation communication where having a cyberchild to deal with is actually an *advantage.* Kids who spend lots of time with computers have a solid understanding of what rules are, how they work, why they're needed, and what can happen when rules are broken. If they're involved in online *communication* (for e-mail, bulletin boards, and users' groups, for instance), these children know everything there is to *know* about conversational turn-taking. They will be able to follow the "Language is traffic" metaphor instantly, and their online communication experience gives them *two* language systems that parallel the traffic on the road. In the same way that the father in Dialogue 1 (p. 24) can ask his child, "What would happen if you tried that kind of behavior on the road?", you can ask a cyberchild, "What would happen if you tried that kind of behavior on the computer?" This is a very useful extra resource.

"Manners" have turned out to be more indispensable online than when talking face to face, because unless everybody follows the rules nobody can interact at *all.* Cyberkids are totally united in their scorn for people who won't cooperate to keep the information moving.

Unless you *are* a cyberperson, you have to let these children know you're *not* one and can't be expected to communicate like one. We now have a three-part transportation system that includes moving people and things by road traffic, moving information by speech and by language on paper, and moving information by language on computer. The three parts use almost the same rules, but the *conditions* are different. Cyberkids are used to having things happen very fast, because that's how computers respond; they get impatient when you can't give them answers as fast as the computer can. They're used to every answer they get being correct down to the last decimal point, and they may demand the same perfection from people they talk to offline.

The best way for adults to deal with this situation is to make it clear in computer language, to take advantage of the power of metaphor. That doesn't mean learning dozens of specialized words and phrases — just a few very basic ones are enough. Here are a few examples:

To say: "Wait a minute, I can't keep track of all that in my head!
           I need to write it down and take a look at it!"
Say this: "Wait a minute! I've only got 16K!"

To say: "Hey — I'm not a computer, I'm a human being!"
Say this: "Hey — which do you think I am, a PC or a Macintosh?"

To say: "What kind of talk is that supposed to be? Keep a civil
           tongue in your head when you talk to me, please."
Say this: "I don't appreciate being <u>flamed</u>; cut it out, please."

To say: "If you keep on like that, you're going to make me so
           angry that this discussion will be <u>over.</u> "
Say this: "If you keep on like that, you'll <u>crash</u> this file."

And when the cyberkids try to carry on three conversations with you at the same time — or two with a friend and one with you at the same time, or any other such combination — remind them that Windows software isn't stored on your disk and you don't *do* parallel processing.

✦

CHAPTER 2

If you REALLY loved me,
YOU'D let me do whatever I WANT!

Managing the English Verbal Attack Patterns

Scenario Two

"So! What are you going to do after you graduate?" asked Will Marcellan. "If you want any kind of chance to get ahead in this world, you have got to stop fiddling around and make some hard decisions!" Beside him on the couch, Marian nodded and leaned toward her daughter, saying, "We really have to know, honey. We have to start making plans."

Kimberly looked at her parents, and quickly looked away again. "WHY are you ALways BUGging me like this?" she demanded. "What's the big RUSH? WHY can't _____"

"The big RUSH," Will cut in, "is that you're only six weeks away from GRADUAtion! Kimberly, suppose you only take NIGHT classes; you STILL have to apPLY! You can't just decide the night before they START!"

"I don't care about that nerdy stuff," the girl muttered. "It's so BORing! It _____"

Will took a deep breath. "Boring or not," he said grimly, "you have to deCIDE. What's it going to be: college or a job? And if it's going to be college, which one?"

"I've told you," Kimberly said sullenly. "I'm not going to get a job, and I'm not going to go to college. PERiod!"

"But KIMberly, that's all there IS!" Marian objected. "This is the

REAL WORLD, honey! And in the real world, you _____ ”

"If you CARED anything aBOUT me," said the teenager, talking so fast that the words tumbled over each other, "YOU'D want me to be HAPpy! DON'T you even CARE if you're RUINing my WHOLE last YEAR of SCHOOL? The ONly senior year I'll ever HAVE? Doesn't that mean ANYthing to you two at ALL?"

"We are NOT ruining your senior year!" Will said, outraged. "That's a riDICulous thing to say! WHY can't you ever THINK before you open your mouth?"

"Oh, yes, you ARE ruining it!" Kimberly shot back at him. "I want to hang out with my FRIENDS and have FUN! That's what kids are SUPPOSED to do! EVen people YOUR age ought to be smart enough to know THAT! YOU keep talking about my 'FUture' — YOU don't really care about that, and you don't care about ME! YOU just want to lay your POWER trips on me, THAT'S all!"

"Kimberly, please!" Marian pleaded. "You're our CHILD, and we LOVE you! But _____ ”

"If I'm only a CHILD," her daughter shouted, "why do I have to talk about stupid COLlege and stupid JOBS? THAT stuff is for OLD people and DWEEBS!"

◆

What's Going On Here?

*Every*thing has gone wrong in Scenario Two. The Marcellans had a plan for this weekend morning. They were going to sit down with their seventeen-year-old daughter for some straight talk about her future. They had two goals: to get a commitment from Kimberly for work or for college, so planning could begin for one or the other, and to make her understand that she can't just go on indefinitely "hanging out and having fun." Will and Marian had their facts and their arguments ready. They knew exactly how the discussion was supposed to go. But it didn't happen that way; they just found themselves in yet one more ugly fight with their daughter.

You'll have noticed that the Marcellans aren't following the language traffic rules, which always makes things difficult. If they'd change that, they'd have a better chance to do some useful talking.

But traffic violations aren't the only problem we see in the scenario; something else is happening.

The Marcellans are all tangled up in a classic language mess based on the *English verbal attack patterns.* We know these patterns in exactly the same way we know the patterns for English questions and commands and threats and promises, because they're part of our grammar. The Marcellan family has *no* chance for successful communication unless they learn how to get these patterns out of their language environment.

What to Do About It— Managing the Verbal Attack Patterns

Let's start by looking carefully at four of the most common verbal attack patterns (VAPs, for short) to understand how we recognize them and how we can respond to them effectively.

Knowing VAPs When We Hear Them

1. "WHY are you always BUGGing me like this?"

"WHY can't you ever THINK before you open your mouth?"

MORE OF THE SAME, FROM ADULTS

"WHY can't you EVer do anything RIGHT?"

"WHY can't you EVer get home on TIME? WHY are you ALways LATE?"

"WHY don't you ever think about what OTHER people might want?"

"WHY do you ALways look like you've slept in your CLOTHES?"

"WHY do you ALways throw your tantrums in the STORE?"

MORE OF THE SAME, FROM CHILDREN

"WHY don't you ever cook anything that TASTES good?"

"WHY do you ALways make me DRESS like a CREEP?"

"WHY are you always so MEAN to me?"

"WHY you NEVer let me go WIF you?"

(As you can see, the more extra stresses on words and parts of words a VAP has, the more hostile and abusive it is.)

2. "If you CARED anything ABOUT me, YOU'D want me to be HAPpy!"

MORE OF THE SAME, FROM ADULTS

"If you REALLY loved me, YOU wouldn't TALK to me like that!"

"If you actually CARED about passing this course, you'd TURN your WORK in on TIME!"

"If you were SERIous about getting a job, YOU wouldn't dress like a THUG!"

"If you really WANTED to make the team, YOU wouldn't keep skipping PRACtice!"

MORE OF THE SAME, FROM CHILDREN

"If you really LOVED us kids, YOU wouldn't WANT to work!"

"If you REALLY loved me, you'd GIVE me a decent ALLOWance!"

"If you really underSTOOD anything about KIDS, you'd BUY me those SNEAKers!"

"If you really WANTED me to get a job, you wouldn't make me wear these STUPid SHOES!"

3. "DON'T you even CARE if you're RUINing my WHOLE last YEAR of SCHOOL?"

MORE OF THE SAME, FROM ADULTS

"DON'T you even CARE if you're BREAKing your mother's HEART?"

"Don't you even CARE IF YOU'RE FAILING SEVENTH GRADE?"

"DON'T you even CARE what people are SAYING ABOUT YOU?"

"DON'T you eve CARE if those cigarettes are ruining your HEALTH?"

MORE OF THE SAME, FROM CHILDREN

"DON'T you even CARE if EVERY kid in my CLASS is LAUGHING AT ME?"

"Don't you even CARE if you're BREAKING my HEART?"

"DON'T you even CARE about my GRADES?"

"DON'T you even CARE about world HUNGER?"

4. "EVen people YOUR age ought to be smart enough to know THAT!"

MORE OF THE SAME, FROM ADULTS:

"EVen a KID should be able to understand that money doesn't grow on TREES!"

"EVen a GIRL could pass THAT class!"

"EVen a CHILD should have SOME sense!"

"EVen a SOPHOmore ought to know enough to stay off DRUGS!"

MORE OF THE SAME, FROM CHILDREN

"EVen GROWNups should know SOMEthing about rap music!"

"EVen an OLD person could understand THAT book!"

"EVEN a person who dresses like a DWEEB should realize that NORmal people CARE about clothes!"

There are more — maybe twenty or so — of these patterns. The four we've just looked at are typical, and I know you had no trouble recognizing them. I am absolutely positive that the VAPs make up at least half of the verbal abuse that most of us face every day. I know for sure that if we could just get rid of *them*, it would go a long way toward making our lives, and our children's lives, better.

Why should we care about this? People sometimes say to me, "So the VAPs hurt . . . so what? After all, they're only *words*; nobody's *hitting* anybody. What's the big deal?" I'm sure we should care; I'm sure these patterns ARE a big deal. But don't just take my word for it.

> Words can hit as hard as a fist.
>
> (National Committee for Prevention of Child Abuse)
>
> Words can be as abusive as physical blows — and their effect can last a lifetime.
>
> (Dr. Joyce Brothers, 1994)
>
> We must remember that injured feelings can be much more lastingly hurtful than physical pain.
>
> (Bruno Bettelheim, 1985)

Many people who would *never* abuse a youngster physically, and who look down on people who do, hand out verbal abuse as if it were completely harmless. Many people who would never call their children vulgar names or yell curses at them will verbally abuse kids as if it were completely safe to do so. *They're mistaken.* The VAPs are the linguistic equivalent of toxic waste, and one of the first things adults can do to clean up the language environment is to get *rid* of them. They're not the only kind of verbal abuse, of course. Any sentence, any sentence at all, can be verbal violence; body language can turn even the words "I love you with all my heart" into sarcasm and abuse. But the VAPs are such a *convenient* way to package hostile language that they get a tremendous amount of use. Here are three specific characteristics that help us recognize them:

✦ CHARACTERISTIC ONE: A VAP always has two parts: the openly hostile chunk that I call the *bait,* and one or more hostile chunks that are harder to spot because they're sheltered.

For example:

"If you really LOVED me, YOU wouldn't TREAT me like DIRT!"

BAIT (OPEN ABUSE)

"You treat me like dirt."

PRESUPPOSED (SHELTERED) ABUSE

"You don't really love me."

In some of the VAPs the separation between the bait and the sheltered attack is very obvious; the "If you REALLY _____" pattern is one of those. In other VAPs the two parts are mixed up together in complicated ways. Children learn the simpler VAPs first. We hear them, I'm sorry to say, from kids as young as two or three. As in, "If you were a REAL mommy, YOU'D let me stay UP!"

Because the word "presupposition" is used with several different meanings, I want to make its use in this book clear. In the *Gentle Art of Verbal Self-Defense* system, *a presupposition is anything a native speaker of the language knows is part of the meaning of an utterance even when it doesn't appear on the surface.* For example:

"Johnny has stopped complaining about his allowance."

When fluent speakers of English hear this sentence, they know that it can only be true if three other sentences are also true:

1. There is a person named Johnny; he exists.

2. Johnny gets an allowance.

3. Johnny, at some time in the past, started complaining about his allowance.

But we don't have to say all those things. If we did, the example sentence would have to read something like this: "Johnny, who exists, has stopped complaining about his allowance, which is something he gets and something that he started complaining about at some time in the past." It would be terribly hard work if we had to talk that way, and it would take forever! We *know* sentences 1–3 are part of the meaning of "Johnny has stopped complaining about his allowance," even though they "aren't there" in the original sentence. This demonstrates that they're presupposed by the speaker. That is, they can be taken for granted unless the speaker is lying or mistaken. If this seems absurdly obvious to you, you're right; that's the point.

✦ CHARACTERISTIC TWO: Although certain words tend to show up more commonly in particular VAPs than other words, it's not the *words* that make the utterance a VAP. It's the tune the words are set to, with all the extra stresses on words and parts of words.

Consider the "If you REALLY . . ." pattern. Here are eight sentences that are all examples of that pattern:

1. "If you REALLY loved me, YOU wouldn't PICK on me!"

2. "If you really LOVED me, you wouldn't PICK on me!"

3. "If you really CARED about me, YOU wouldn't PICK on me!"

4. "If you felt a GENuine love for me, YOU wouldn't misTREAT me!"

5. "If I really MATTERED to you, you wouldn't misTREAT me!"

6. "YOU wouldn't PICK on me if you REALLY loved me!"

7. "If what you felt for me was really LOVE, you wouldn't be so incredibly MEAN to me!"

8. "People who really LOVE people don't PICK on them!"

We recognize these as VAPs by what they have in common, even when the words — and the *positions* of the extra stresses — are different.

When somebody puts stress on "sixty" in "It wasn't forty dollars, it was <u>sixty</u> dollars!" that stress is needed to contrast "forty" with "sixty." It's not extra, it's required. The stress on "won" and "sweep" in "I WON the SWEEPstakes!" isn't extra; the speaker needs it to carry the metamessage of surprise and excitement. But the extra emphatic stresses in the VAPs aren't there for contrast, or to help make announcements about amazing events. They're there for just one reason, *to carry hostile messages,* and your internal grammar is perfectly capable of spotting them in spite of the varied forms they may take.

✦ CHARACTERISTIC THREE: People who use a VAP are almost never interested in the response they'd get if their words were a *neutral* statement or question.

Let's look at two questions that contain exactly the same words but don't mean the same thing at all, because the words are set to very different tunes.

1. "Why are you reading that book?"

This is a question from someone who wants to know the answer and expects a response like "Because there's nothing else to read in this house" or "Because I have to write a book report about it in Mrs. Jacoby's class" or "Because it's exciting and I like the characters."

2. "WHY are you READing THAT BOOK?"

If the person asking question 2 is interested in the reason for reading the book, it's a coincidence. This sentence is an attack. The most likely response to it is something like, "Listen, I have a right to read whatEVER I WANT to read! What business is it of YOURS why I'm reading it?" At best, the response will be something like, "Because I HAVE to write a BOOK report about it, THAT'S why!" And answers like those are what the questioner is expecting.

Clearly the anger can't be a reaction to the words — the words in the two examples are exactly the same. The reaction is to the body language — especially to the tune the words are set to.

Let's look at two dialogues to see what a difference the tunes can make in the way an interaction turns out.

DIALOGUE 4

Father: "Why are you leaving?"

Teen: "Because I've got to catch the schoolbus, Dad."

Father: "Oh, sure! I forgot it was Monday."

Another way this might have happened is:

DIALOGUE 4 REVISITED

Father: "WHY are YOU LEAVing?"

Teen: "Whadda you _mean_, why am I leaving? I ALways leave at 7:30, Dad! I'D miss the BUS if I DIDn't!"

Father: "Well, you DON'T have to get SMART about it!"

Teen: "THAT'S NOT FAIR! YOU STARTED it!"

Father: "YOU WATCH YOUR MOUTH, young man!"

The father's opening line in Dialogue 4, "Why are you leaving?", presupposes something like "You have a piece of information that I'm interested in, and I'm asking you to share it with me." But in Dialogue 4 Revisited the heavily stressed "Why" adds one more presupposition: "And I'm warning you in advance: No matter WHAT your answer is, it isn't GOOD enough!" The extra stresses on "you" and "leav-" add messages of anger and hostility. The teenager in this dialogue hears those messages and, very naturally, is hostile right *back*. The result is a fight — and a bad start to the morning for both the adult and the child.

Don't worry about the lack of space to analyze all of the English VAPs in detail here. You don't need all that explanation. The VAPs are part of your grammar; you've recognized them and used them yourself since you were a small child. I haven't been telling you anything you didn't know; I've just organized information you already have, in a way that gives you reliable and efficient *access* to it. You'll be able to apply it to any VAP that comes your way.

Now let's move on to discuss the best method for *responding* to the verbal attack patterns.

Responding to the Verbal Attack Patterns

Answers to the English VAPs should be based on these two *Gentle Art* metaprinciples:

* Remember that anything you feed will grow.

* Do everything you honorably can to avoid causing loss of face.

Since using any VAP sets up one end of a *hostility loop,* what's needed is a response that (a) doesn't *feed* that loop, (b) is appropriate for the interaction, and (c) will cause no loss of face on either side.

In the same way that the traffic metaphor is valuable for explaining how conversations work, a fishing metaphor will help us understand (and explain) the verbal attack patterns. When you go fishing, you expect the fish to take your *bait*. You'd be amazed if the fish grabbed your fishing rod or your boots instead, and it would seriously disrupt the plans you had for catching that fish. Similarly, verbal attackers expect their listeners to take the bait in a VAP and respond to it directly; anything else is going to surprise them and wreck their plans. The right move, therefore, is to *ignore* the bait, no matter how tempting it may be, and respond directly to a presupposed part of the attack.

To make this more clear, let's look at a pair of dialogues. The verbal attacker is a nine-year-old boy; here's the VAP he will use, and its parts:

"If you REALLY wanted me to get good grades, YOU'D buy me a comPUTer like all the OTHER kids have got!"

BAIT

"All the other kids have computers except me."

PRESUPPOSED ATTACK

"You don't really want me to get good grades."

DIALOGUE 5: When the Adult Takes the Bait

Child: "If you REALLY wanted me to get good grades, YOU'D buy me a comPUTer, like all the OTHER kids have got!"

Father: "Oh, come ON! All the other kids do NOT have computers!"

Child   "They do, too! EVerybody has one but ME!"

Father: "Tommy doesn't have a computer."

Child: "Yes, he DOES! He has it in his BEDroom!"

Father: "Well, if he does, he only JUST GOT it! And I KNOW MARK doesn't have one!"

Child: "Oh, yes he DOES! You just don't KNOW! I was at his house YESterday, and he _____ "

(And so on, through the list of the child's friends, until the father's patience is exhausted.)

DIALOGUE 5 REVISITED: When the Adult Ignores the Bait

Child: "If you REALLY wanted me to get good grades, YOU'D buy me a comPUTer, like all the OTHER kids have got!"

Father: "When did you start thinking that I don't want you to get good grades?"

Child: "Well . . . I . . . "

Father: "Of course I want you to get good grades. That's very important to me, and to your mother. And we know you can do it, too. Don't you think so?"

Child: "I dunno . . . Maybe."

Father: "Which one of your classes is worrying you right now?"

Child: "Spelling is really <u>hard</u>, Dad . . . I keep getting it <u>wrong</u>."

Father: "How about getting your spelling book and showing me? Maybe I can help."

You see how this works? The child goes into the interaction expecting his dad to take the bait and argue with him about whether all the others kids have computers or not; he's prepared for that. He has all his facts and arguments ready. (He'll also be ready to argue about whether kids have to have a computer to get good grades, if his father takes that road.) But he takes it for granted that the adult *will* go for the bait and that the sheltered attack—"You don't care whether I get good grades or not!"—will slip right by without challenge. When that does happen (Dialogue 5), the child gets the fight he was after. When it *doesn't* happen (Dialogue 5 Revisited), the child is completely at a loss! He has nothing to fuel the hostility loop he'd planned to set up, and the best he can do is a baffled "Well . . . I . . . "

Here's one more example of this technique. The two VAPs children usually begin using first are the "If you REALLY . . . ." pattern and the "WHY do you ALWAYS/WHY don't you EVER . . . " pattern. Here's the VAP for our example, in which the attacker is a nine-year-old girl.

"WHY do we ALWAYS have to go where YOU want to go? WHY don't you ever take me someplace that's for KIDS?"

BAIT

"You never take me anywhere that's intended for children; you only take me to places that are meant for grownups like you."

PRESUPPOSED ATTACKS

"Whatever your answer to this question is, it's not good enough."

"There are absolutely no exceptions to what I'm accusing you of."

DIALOGUE 6: When the Adult Takes the Bait

Child: "WHY do we ALWAYS have to go where YOU want to go? WHY don't you ever take me someplace that's for KIDS?"

Father: "That's riDICulous! I took you to DISNEYland! Remember that? I suppose DISneyland isn't for KIDS!"

Child: "That was last summer . . . that was a LONG TIME ago!"

Father: "Summer was NOT a long time ago. It's only NoVEMber!"

Child: "Well, Disneyland is the ONly neat place we ever went to! All the OTHER times, we had to go to the dumb old REStaurant!"

Father: "That's not TRUE. I took you to the museum, I took you to _____ "

Child: "The MUSEUM's not for kids! It's STUPid!"

Father: "What do you MEAN, it's stupid! It's got dinosaurs, it's got _____ "

(And so on, through the list of places this man has taken his daughter, until his patience is exhausted.)

DIALOGUE 6 REVISITED: When the Adult Ignores the Bait

Child: "WHY do we ALWAYS have to go where YOU want to go? WHY don't you ever take me someplace that's for KIDS?"

Father: "Okay — let's go to the museum again. We can look at that dinosaur exhibit."

Child: "I don't WANT to go the museum!"

Father   "All right, we don't have to."

Child: "Well . . . where <u>are</u> we going to go, Daddy?"

Father: "I don't know. It's hard to decide. Do you have any good ideas?"

Child: "Jenny's daddy took her to the lake, and they went for a ride on a big <u>boat</u>."

The father's strategy here is a response to the presupposition that there are no exceptions to his daughter's accusation. He proves that false *on the spot* by suggesting that they go see the dinosaur exhibit. If she'd been pleased by that choice, he would have agreed to take her there. When she isn't pleased, he immediately says — neutrally, without sarcasm — that they don't have to go there. With either reaction from the child, he immediately demonstrates that her presupposition is false: They do not always have to go only to places where *he* wants to go.

At this point you may be thinking, *But he's letting her get away with <u>mur</u>der!* He's letting her push him <u>around</u>! Your reaction is natural; it comes from your long years of experience playing this particular language game and assuming that there's no other way to handle it. It's a misunderstanding of what's actually going on.

This little girl had a plan: Her father would spend the next fifteen or twenty minutes fighting with her, involved in a ridiculous argument with her, giving her his complete and undivided attention — instead of doing whatever *he* had planned to do with that segment of his time. Her plan worked, for the father in Dialogue 6: *She got away with it.* The father in Dialogue 6 Revisited didn't let that happen. He could of course have achieved that same result this way:

DIALOGUE 6A: Laying Down the Law

Child: "WHY do we ALWAYS have to go someplace YOU want to go? WHY can't we ever go someplace that's for KIDS?"

Father: "One more word out of YOU, young lady, and we won't go ANYwhere!"

That's one way of doing it, sure. If the adult's goal is to maintain military discipline in the home, that's the kind of strategy he needs to use. But if his goal is to help the child develop good communication skills, it's a poor choice. It has two serious drawbacks:

First: It orders the child to maintain complete silence.

If she obeys him, the interaction is over; that's not conversation. If she doesn't, either the outing together is canceled or he's made an empty threat, and neither of those outcomes is a good idea. He has left her *no* good choice.

Second: It causes the child to lose face, which means she will feel *obligated* to make a show of resistance.

This child knows she won't get anywhere resisting, because her father has all the power in the situation, and will put her down again. But because the interaction has been set up as one that has to end with a winner and a loser—and because she lives in a society that honors winners and looks down on losers—she'll feel that she has to *try* to be the winner, even though she knows she'll lose. And when she does lose, her resentment of her father, with all the communication barriers that causes, will grow.

The father in Dialogue 6 Revisited has made the best choice. He hasn't let his child sucker him into a long verbal struggle that can only turn out badly while at the same time demonstrating her power to control *his* behavior. He hasn't caused his child to lose face by demonstrating something that needs no demonstration—that he is bigger and stronger and has more power in the long run than she has. He has changed the situation from a confrontation to a friendly discussion. He can still stop at any point and give orders, if necessary; that's one of the *advantages* of talking to a child rather than to another adult. He's in control of what's happening, but he's giving the child plenty of room to learn about negotiation and conversation. And he isn't building up feelings of resentment in either himself *or* the child. This is much better.

To understand how we got to this conclusion, we need to

answer one more question about the verbal attack patterns: What are they *for*?

Why People Use the Verbal Attack Patterns

Very small children may use a VAP only because they've heard others use it, without realizing that the result is almost sure to be unpleasant. That's a very short stage; it doesn't last. Adults who are overtired and overstressed because of a hopelessly awful day may use a VAP only as a symptom that they're human and have limits. But that doesn't last either; it's a temporary problem. Occasional rare VAP attacks aren't significant. But people who use VAPs frequently and consistently do so for very reliable reasons. Children learn the grammar of verbal violence by observation, using their inborn ability to figure out rules from raw data in their language environment, just like any other part of the grammar. Once they understand the VAPping process (typically by the time they're five, and often much sooner), they use VAPs for the same purpose as the adults they've learned it from.

The verbal attack patterns are *action chains*. That is: They're made up of specific steps that have to happen in a specific order, or the attack fails. Like this:

STEP ONE

The attacker throws out a VAP.

STEP TWO

The intended victim takes the bait and runs with it.

STEP THREE

Attacker and victim exchange unpleasant chunks of language until one of them gives up.

The most important thing to remember is that *any time this sequence takes place, the attacker wins.* Even if the two people involved are an adult and a child. Even if, because the victim is an adult with the power to punish, the attack ends with the child being spanked or having to surrender the car keys. When the intended victim takes the bait and participates in the exchange of hostilities — which is what the attacker has in mind — the attacker wins.

People use the verbal attack patterns to achieve these goals:

- To demonstrate their power to get and keep the victim's attention.

- To get an emotional reaction from the victim that is additional evidence of that power.

This is the critical information you have to have for managing the VAPs. Ordinarily, people make statements because they're interested in hearing what reasonable people would say back. Ordinarily, people ask questions because they're interested in the answers. But people who use VAPs frequently and consistently, people who routinely *start* language interactions with a VAP, have a different agenda. What they want is attention, and proof of their power to get and keep attention.

This is just as true of children as it is of adults. It's normal for youngsters to want the attention of the adults around them and to work hard to get it. *If the technique of using VAPs for that purpose is modeled for them, they learn it and they use it.*

Once you understand the verbal attacker's purpose, once you understand that the bait is outrageous because the attacker (like a person who goes fishing) wants it to be as tempting — as attention getting — as possible, you'll be able to look at the whole process with the detachment it deserves. It won't be possible for VAPpers to just push your buttons and make you react automatically.

The rules for responding to VAPs are:

✦ RULE ONE: Ignore the bait — no matter how tempting.

✦ RULE TWO: Respond directly to a presupposition.

✦ RULE THREE: Whatever you do, transmit this message:

"You're wasting your time trying that with me; I won't play that game."

You can set aside the sentimental idea that children aren't able to use linguistic strategies like the VAPs. Kids are at the *peak* of their language-learning powers, better at them than they'll ever be again. That's why it's so much easier for young children to become fluent speakers of a foreign language than for their parents to. In most activities where adults are measured against children, the adults are so far ahead that measuring isn't *fair*. But language learning is unique; it's the one kind of learning for which children have a genuine advantage. Children who spend their time with adults who use the VAPs to do verbal violence tangos can be counted on to extract the rules from the data they observe, swiftly and expertly. It's humbling to watch tiny kids suckering adults into VAP matches; they are *very* good at it. And every time it works, they learn from that and get better and better at it.

Body Language and the English VAPs

The VAPs *depend* on body language — only the intonation with which they're spoken makes them attacks. The difference between "Why did you say that?" and "WHY did you SAY that?" is the tune the words are set to, which is the result of such things as greater tension in the vocal tract muscles. The facial expression and gestures may be different, too, but you know you're under attack when you hear "WHY did you SAY that?" on the telephone. This demonstrates that it's the intonation of the voice that matters most.

The rest of the body language works *with* the intonation to help the attacker indicate how *intense* the attack is. A VAP that's said with a scowl on the speaker's face, or while the speaker's fist punches at the air, will be understood as more intense and more hostile than a VAP that doesn't have that kind of physical "punctuation and graphics."

Here is a set of sample dialogues that will help make all of this information clearer.

Sample Dialogues

DIALOGUE 7 (to a second-grade class)

Teacher: "All right, class, let's get ready for the test."

Child 1:   "Oh, NO!"

Child 2:   "Do we HAVE TO?"

Teacher: "Oh, you don't need to be worried. <u>EV</u>en the <u>first</u> graders can pass <u>this</u> test!"

This adult isn't attacking the children, and has the best of intentions. But there's a problem. One of the most common English VAPs is the one that begins with "EVen a(n) . . ." as in, "EVen a TEENager could pass THIS course!" or, "EVen a TEACHer can balance a CHECKbook!" As a result, the line that's intended to make the kids feel better will actually make their anxiety worse. Let's look at it more closely to see why. It has two parts.

1. "<u>EV</u>en the <u>first</u> graders _____"

This chunk presupposes, mildly, that first graders are in some way inferior. ("EVen the FIRST graders _____" would presuppose it more strongly.) The teacher's *intention* is to endorse the second-grade children's perceptions of themselves as wiser and more sophisticated than the first graders, to give them confidence. But the presupposition is built into the language; it insults the younger children, and the older ones understand that. Second-graders who don't pass the test will have to deal with the fact that they couldn't do something their teacher said could be done by kids the teacher thinks are *inferior* to second-graders. Adults who say things like "EVen a BABY can do that!" or "EVen a BABY can do THAT!" need to realize that they're saying, "I don't have much respect for babies, and if you can't do [whatever], I respect you even less than I respect <u>them</u>."

2. "_____ can pass <u>this</u> test!"

The extra stress on "this" signals another presupposition: that the test itself is so trivial that it's hardly worth taking. A child who fails it has been told that it's a test only a really *stupid* second-grader would fail.

Suppose we expanded that sentence to make its presuppositions show up on the surface. It would then look like this:

"<u>E</u>ven the <u>first</u>-graders (who, as everybody knows, can barely find the playground by themselves) can pass <u>this</u> test (which, as everybody knows, is so trivial and silly that nobody with half a brain could fail it.")

Children who speak English hear all that additional layer of meaning. Whether they're consciously aware of it or not, the presupposed information is understood. What the teacher *intended* isn't the point; the children will use what they understand the teacher to mean as the basis for their behavior. An adult who wants to give children confidence to help them do well on a test should just say, "I think you'll do well on this. I know I can count on you to do your very best."

DIALOGUE 8 (with a fourteen-year-old girl)

Teen: "Mom, can I have a San Andreas Faultfinders CD for my birthday?"

Adult: "A what? What's a San Andreas Faultfinder?"

Teen: "<u>H</u>onestly, Mother!" <u>E</u>ven a woman <u>your</u> age ought to know SOMEthing about music!"

Adult: "Oh, <u>real</u>ly! <u>Listen</u>, young lady, <u>I</u> know more about music than <u>you</u> will EVer know!"

This exchange will now turn into a fight over what the mother does and doesn't know about music, what is and what isn't music, and more. The teenager started it by throwing out an example of the "EVen a(n) _____" VAP: "<u>E</u>ven a person <u>your</u> age ought to know SOMEthing about music!" And the adult—who ought to know better—immediately took her up on the offer to play Abuser & Victim by grabbing the bait and running with it. Here's an alternate version.

DIALOGUE 8 REVISITED

Teen: "Mom, can I have a San Andreas Faultfinders CD for my birthday?"

Adult: "A what? What's a San Andreas Faultfinder?"

Teen: "Honestly, Mother!" Even a woman your age ought to know SOMEthing about music!"

Adult: "The idea that there's something wrong with being a woman my age is one you hear once in a while . . . I'm surprised to hear it from you. Now tell me the name of that CD again, so we can talk about whether to get it for your birthday."

The adult has said quite clearly: "I notice that you want to start a fight; I hear the insult about women my age. You're wasting your time. I won't play that stupid game." If the child wants a fight, she'll have to start a new one; this one is over. Notice that the adult has kept her intonation neutral. If she had said, "I'm surPRISED to hear it from YOU!", with the same words but a different tune, that would have been a counterattack.

DIALOGUE 9 (with a twelve-year-old child)

Child: "Teachers who CARE about their students try to make the lessons INTeresting!"

Teacher: "You're absolutely right."

This interaction is very short, and that's as it should be. The child expected the teacher to say, "Listen here, I DO try to make my lessons interesting!" or, "I beg your pardon! Just what is THAT supposed to mean? I DO care about my students!!" Followed, in either case, by an argument. When that didn't happen, the attack failed, and the next move is up to the youngster.

This child's VAP is a skillful variation on, "If you really CARED about your students, YOU'D make your lessons INTeresting!" But the way it's put together includes a presupposition that there *do exist* some hypothetical teachers who care about their students and try to make their lessons interesting. The adult in the dialogue has responded to *that* presupposition instead of taking the bait. Whenever you can end an attack by agreeing with an irrelevant presupposition and there's no reason *not* to do so, it's the best possible move.

DIALOGUE 10 (with a twelve-year-old girl)

Child: "GROSS! I can't stand it! Why do we have to have have her in our house? Why can't she go stay in a nursing home like all the other old ladies?!"

Adult: "Shame on you! You're talking about your grandmother!"

Child: "So? She's still an old lady, and if she moves in with us it'll ruin my whole LIFE!"

Adult: "Your grandmother has always been good to you, and she loves you very very much. And you love her, too. After she's been here a week or two and we've all had time to get used to _____ "

Child: "I don't love her!"

Adult: "Of course you do! She's your grandmother!"

Child: "I don't CARE! I DON'T love her, and I don't want her LIVING here! If she moves in, don't expect ME to talk to her and be nice and stuff! Just forGET THAT!"

Adult: "(*Icily.*) You . . . are . . . disgusting. GO to your room!"

The adult in this dialogue is following a traditional script based on the idea that love follows automatically from close kinship and that having an elderly person move into your home is no big deal. Both of those ideas are romantic myths, and the adult who pretends otherwise is headed for serious trouble. I suggest this version:

DIALOGUE 10 REVISITED

Child: "GROSS! I can't stand it! Why do we have to have her in our house? Why can't she go stay in a nursing home like all the other old ladies?!"

Adult: "Sometimes bringing an elderly person into the house doesn't work out. Sometimes it makes everybody — including that person — so miserable that the only good solution is a nursing home. I know that. But I'd rather have your grandmother here with us."

Child: "WHY? It's gonna be AWful! WHY?"

Adult: "Because she is my mother, and I enjoy her company."

Child: "That's CRAzy!"

Adult: "Some parents and children don't get along, some do. It's not automatic. Grandmother Ann and I have always enjoyed being together, and I see no reason why she should have to live with strangers when we have two extra bedrooms."

Child: "If she moves in here, don't expect me to pretend that I'M happy about it! I don't WANT her here!"

Adult: "You're under no obligation to smother your grandmother with love and kisses. You do have to be polite and respectful to her; I know I can count on you for that. Let's try it; let's give it a chance and see how it goes."

In this version the adult uses straight talk and acknowledges that in the real world it may change your life in drastic ways to have someone move into your home. The adult is careful not to *shame* the child, because the grandmother would be blamed for that too.

And instead of ordering the child to act loving, instead of saying, "Oh yes you WILL pretend that you're happy your grandmother is here with us!", this adult uses the power of presupposition. Saying "I know I can count on you to be polite and respectful," compliments the child. It avoids the direct command while still clearly stating what's expected. This is good communication strategy. What's needed here is the child's cooperation; if that cooperation comes only from threats, the child will resent it bitterly and will take it out on the grandparent and everyone else in the house. Any time the topic of a discussion is as sensitive as this one, language should be kept as neutral as possible — so that *more* strong emotions don't get tossed into the mix and make matters even worse.

DIALOGUE 11 (with an eleven-year-old boy)

Adult: "Tell you what—if you pass the <u>math</u> test, we'll go look for that game you've been wanting."

Child: "You mean I can't <u>have</u> it if I don't pass the stupid test? That's not <u>fair</u>! <u>Lots</u> of kids don't pass!"

Adult: "Kids who study don't fail. It's just that simple."

Child: "That's <u>easy</u> for <u>you</u> to say! Anything <u>you</u> want, you just go BUY it!"

Adult: "That's not <u>true</u>!"

Child: "Oh, yeah? What about that new software package you went out and got yesterday?"

Adult: "WHY is it always a waste of time to try to do something nice for you? ExPLAIN that, please!"

Child: "Hey, WHY does everything you say you're gonna DO for me have STRINGS attached? Explain THAT!"

This interaction is only going to go from bad to worse. The child has led the adult down one garden path after another and is unlikely to stop when he's on such a roll. Both speakers are so angry that every word they say is hostile; their last two utterances are VAPs. Is there any obvious explanation for this?

Yes, there is. First, children from about the age of nine are often almost cocked and primed for fights. They will use even the most trivial hint of hostility as an excuse to start one. Second, the adult in this dialogue has set the stage for a confrontation at the very beginning, with this line:

Adult: "Tell you what—if you pass the <u>math</u> test, we'll go look for that game you've been wanting.

The problem here is the word "if." Most of the time, unless it's used *very* carefully, "if" presupposes that something is *not* the case. For example, "If you really *loved* me _____" means "You don't really love me." There are times when "if" is the right choice, as in

"If it rains, we won't be able to go to the beach." But adults shouldn't use "if" to talk about things they hope a child will or won't do. Saying "If you pass the test" sounds too much like "I don't think you'll pass the test," especially to a child who's already worried about it. Instead of "if," use *time* words or phrases that carry no negative meaning, as in these two examples using "after" and "when":

> "Tell you what — after you pass the math test, we'll go look for that game you've been wanting."

> "Tell you what — when you pass the math test, we'll go look for that game you've been wanting."

These sentences presuppose that the child *will* pass the test, and that's much better.

Even with very small children, adults often get into the habit of using "if" utterances to negotiate outcomes the kids shouldn't be *allowed* to haggle over. They say, "If you won't yell when you get your shot _____" and "If you'll go to bed and stay there _____" and "If you'll do the dishes _____" and "If you'll just stop screaming _____," followed by what can only be called a bribe, such as "I'll buy you a candy bar." The end result is the following message:

> "I don't think you're going to do this. But suppose I'm wrong. Suppose you surprise me and you <u>do</u> it. If that happens, I'll reward you."

Obviously that's bad strategy! You need to use language that gives a message of your confidence in the child and presupposes that the desired behavior can be taken for granted. Here are some examples that tell children "I think you can do it" and don't make them feel as though they have to put up a fight.

> "When you get your shot without yelling, I'm very proud of you."

> "When you go to bed and stay there without whining, you set a good example for your little sister."

"After you do the dishes, I'll be able to start dinner."

"When you're through with the dishes, we can watch the game."

"While you're doing the dishes, you could be thinking about which of the football games would be best to watch tonight. I can't make up my mind."

Finally, when adults propose that children do things they *know* the kids will object to, they can offer what is called "an illusion of choice" as a face-preserving measure. Like this:

"After you do the dishes, would you rather we ate right away or do you want to watch television first?"

"While you're doing the dishes, do you want to listen to rock music or would you rather I put on that Joan Baez album?"

When kids hear questions like these, they understand that they're going to have to do the dishes. Of course. But adults who use these questions are also showing the children how one person can let another one know that something has to be done, while still treating that person with respect. The same presupposition power that's used so negatively to put VAPs together can also be used to achieve some *positive* goals.

Now let's go back to Scenario Two to see how a skilled handling of the verbal attack patterns could have helped the people involved communicate better.

Another Look at Scenario Two

Will Marcellan's second sentence to his daughter is a classic VAP. He says:

"If you want any kind of chance of to get ahead in this world, you have <u>got</u> to stop fiddling around and make some hard decisions!"

The bait is "All you do is fiddle around, instead of making the hard decisions that you have to make." The presupposed attack is "You don't care anything about getting ahead in this world."

Kimberly doesn't hesitate for a minute; she takes the bait. And we can tell she's had a lot of practice at this game. She doesn't just come back at her father with an automatic "I do NOT just fiddle around! I HAVE been making decisions!" She responds by counter-attacking with a VAP of her own:

"WHY are you always BUGGing me like this?"

Later Kimberly uses the same VAP her father started out with, plus one more:

"If you CARED anything aBOUT me, YOU'D want me to be HAPPy! DON'T you even CARE if you're ruining my WHOLE last YEAR of SCHOOL?"

Her father instantly takes the bait and snaps back with "We are NOT ruining your senior year! That's a riDICulous thing to say!" He finishes off his turn with the first VAP Kimberly tried on him, saying, "WHY can't you ever THINK before you open your mouth?"

You can't miss it: These are people who are used to wasting their time working their way through one bout after another of the VAP-ping game. They say almost nothing in the entire scenario that's *not* an example of a verbal attack pattern, and the language that surrounds the VAPs backs them up by being almost totally hostile.

It doesn't have to be like this. Suppose Will opens with the attack shown, but Kimberly doesn't take the bait . . .

Will: "If you want to have any chance to get <u>ahead</u> in this world, you have <u>got</u> to stop fiddling around and make some hard de<u>cisions</u>!"

Kimberly: "Of course I want to get ahead; that really matters a lot to me."

Will: "I'm sorry — it seemed to me that you weren't thinking about that at all."

Kimberly: "No, Dad, I do think about it. But I don't understand why we have to be in such a hurry."

Now Will and Marian could go ahead and explain to Kimberly about the lead time she needs if she wants to arrange either college or a job.

Suppose that Will begins the discussion *without* a VAP, making only some neutral remark about the need to make decisions now, and it's Kimberly who throws out the first attack. Suppose he then follows the rules for handling VAPs instead of taking her bait . . .

Kimberly: "WHY are you always BUGGing me like this? What's the big RUSH? Why can't you just let me ALONE instead of constantly NAGGING at me?"

Will: "All right. How about doing it this way . . . let's set up a time when we could discuss this. When would you like to do that?"

Kimberly: "I don't <u>ever</u> want to discuss it, Dad. I don't want to talk about it at all! Do we <u>have</u> to?"

Will: "I think so. What do you think, Marian? Is it safe to put off this discussion a while?"

Marian: "No. Too many things that have to be done, and we just don't have much time left to do them."

Will: "Well, then, Kimberly — it's up to you. Let's pick a time when you'd be ready to tackle this."

Kimberly: (*Sighs.*) "We might as well go ahead and get it over with, then."

Will: "That's fine with me. Marian, why don't you start?"

Marian: "The first question we need to talk about, honey, is . . ."

This is still a difficult conversation, between two adults who want their teenager to start taking adult responsibilities and a child who only wants to have a good time. Changing the language doesn't change those facts. But tackling it this way keeps all three of them *on the subject that needs to be discussed.* It keeps them from wasting the entire time they spend talking together, with no chance of any positive outcome.

Unless this happens, nothing *useful* can happen. Families today (and adult–child pairs like teacher and student, doctor and patient, employer and employee) have too little communication time available to waste it in bickering and confrontation and verbal power games. And they have too little communication time for the adults to waste it in showing the children all the *wrong* ways to communicate.

There are three reliable ways to avoid that waste.

✦ FIRST: Be sure you don't throw out any VAPs yourself.

✦ SECOND: If you realize that you're in the middle of a VAP, *stop*. Say, "Wait a minute, I'm doing this all wrong! Let me start this over again."

✦ THIRD: When VAPs are flying and you're the target, follow the rules in this chapter: Ignore the bait, respond to a presupposition, and get the message across that this is a game you aren't willing to play.

Talking to the Cyberchild

Using the verbal attack patterns — VAPping — is a kind of "flaming" (the term for a verbal attack on line); pointing that out may make the cyberchild a little more careful. The most likely VAP from a cyberkid is one like this:

"I'LL bet you don't EVen KNOW what a serial port IS!"

(The computer term may not be "serial port," of course; there are hundreds of other possibilities.)

This attack is built around the most mysterious word in English — the word "even." That "even," especially with an extra stress added, presupposes that anybody ignorant about serial ports is beneath contempt. It's not as complicated as it looks, though; it's just a variation on examples like this one:

"EVen the stupidest person on EARTH would know what a SERial PORT is!"

The presupposed chunk is "The stupidest person on earth would know what a serial port is" and the bait is, "You're stupider than the stupidest person on earth." As always, ignore the bait and respond to a presupposition. Like this:

"The idea that people who aren't familiar with computer terms are stupid is something you hear once in a while; I'm surprised to hear it from you." (Or, "I'm sorry you feel that way.")

✦

CHAPTER 3

When you __act__ like that, __you__ drive me NUTS!

Using Three-Part Messages

Scenario Three

Harriet Lassiter knew everybody in the restaurant was looking at her and at her family; she didn't blame them a bit. She knew what they were thinking. Especially if they didn't have any kids themselves, or, worse yet, if they had kids that *behaved* in public.

John Lassiter was trying to *threaten* their children into submission; it wasn't working. Harriet bit her lip as eight-year-old Linda answered John's "You settle down, or you're getting a spanking!" with a gay little laugh and a toss of her ponytail. Followed by "You wouldn't dare spank me in public, Daddy! There's a law against it!"

"I can carry you out of here," John told her through clenched teeth, trying to keep his own voice down. "And when I get you out to the car I'll blister your sassy little tail!"

"I'll scream if you do that," Linda answered, with an insufferable smirk on her face, " and everybody will think you're kidnapping me!"

"Linda Charlotte Lassiter," John began, grimly — and then he stopped short as Tommy, the two-year-old, took off running around the table, followed by four-year-old Kathleen.

Harriet grabbed the toddler and John grabbed Kathleen. Each sat holding one struggling child tightly; both kids were screaming at the tops of their lungs. Meanwhile, Linda sat laughing at the spectacle and clapping her hands.

"John," said Harriet quickly, under her breath, "don't yell now! Just tell them, firmly, that they've got to calm down."

"<u>You</u> tell them!" he snapped. "I'm not going to talk to them again until they're <u>thir</u>ty, myself!"

"Oh, <u>Daddy</u>!" Linda caroled. "You are <u>so</u> <u>silly</u>!"

"Linda," Harriet said sternly, "I want you to straighten up, <u>right now</u>! I am disgusted by your behavior, and I want it to <u>stop</u>. <u>Don't</u> make me have to tell you <u>again</u>, young lady!"

"You're not being FAIR!" Linda wailed, tears appearing like magic in her eyes and pouring down over her cheeks. "I'M not the one that was running around the table! I'M being GOOD! YOU ALways pick on MEEEEE!"

"Linda, that's not true," said Harriet. "I've told you a hundred times: you're the <u>big</u> girl in the family! The other kids look <u>up</u> to you, and they _____ "

"<u>Kathleen</u> doesn't," said Linda. "She won't even let me play with her <u>Bar</u>bies."

"That's not the same thing," Harriet objected. "They still _____ "

"Tommy get DOWN!" shrieked the little boy in her lap. "MOMmy! DOWN!"

"I want down TOO, Daddy! PLEEEASE don't hold ON to me!" That was Kathleen.

John and Harriet looked at each other, and they both nodded. leaving now, when they'd already ordered, was going to cost them, but they didn't have any choice. And since it was a lost cause anyway, John made sure he could be heard over his offspring's racket. Putting three ten-dollar bills on the table to cover the check, he stood up, still clutching Kathleen, and announced: "That's it. That's <u>it</u>! From now <u>on</u>, when your mother and I go out, you <u>kids</u> are staying HOME!"

"THAT'S NOT FAIR!" Linda howled as Harriet dragged her and Tommy toward the door. "I HATE you! I HATE you BOTH! And I HATE TOMmy and KathLEEN, TOO!"

Both adults did their best to ignore the cheering from the other diners as the restaurant door closed behind them.

✦

What's Going On Here?

Now and then I meet people who tell me that children aren't capable of verbal abuse. Often they say their claims are based on some scientist's theory about "stages of development" in children. I disagree. I'm willing to go along with the idea that infants under three months or so are linguistically innocent, since I can't prove the contrary, although my own experience with tiny infants who obviously have their parents well trained makes me dubious even about that. But people who think that children old enough to talk can't use language as a weapon only need to watch one mess like the one in Scenario Three to find out how wrong they are.

It *is* true that the younger children are, the harder is it for them to *separate* physical abuse from verbal abuse. The screaming toddler is likely to also be kicking and hitting. Five-year-olds shrieking in full tantrum, but no longer able to get away with kicking and hitting *people,* will fling themselves down and kick and hit the floor or the furniture. Older kids and teenagers will slam doors and throw things during verbal outbursts if they think they can do so safely. It takes a long time to learn the self-control needed to confine the expression of anger and hostility to language alone. Children who don't have plenty of chances to observe adults expressing negative emotions in a controlled and appropriate way won't learn how. And such children are all too likely to grow up and join the other adults responsible for the epidemic of physical violence in our homes today.

The poor Lassiters have a lot of work to do to put their family communication in order. No one tactic would turn them around. But there's a technique they could use to get started, one that's a tremendous help when adults are asking children to change their behavior: *They could learn to use three-part messages.*

What to Do About It—
Using Three-Part Messages

Most children go through predictable stages in the way they resist adult commands, suggestions, and requests:

When they're very small they'll settle for "No!" and "I won't!", relying on volume and dramatics to make up for their weaknesses in vocabulary and strategy.

Next comes pleading and whining, as in "Pleeeeeeease don't MAKE meeeeee!"

Finally, they reach a stage in which their favorite tactic is to seize on some item in an adult utterance and try to sucker the adult into arguing about it. The verbally skilled child will try to set up an argument about something *other than* the change in behavior, hoping that will distract the adult from the main issue.

The Lassiters have a two-year-old child at the "No!" stage, a four-year-old still in transition between "I won't!" and "Pleeeease don't MAKE meeeee!," and an eight-year-old girl who lacks verbal elegance but knows all about using irrelevant arguments for distraction. Whenever Harriet and John want these children to change their behavior in some way, they use two linguistic strategies:

1. Commands, direct or indirect, as in . . .

   "Eat your peas!" (Direct command)
   "I wish you would eat your peas." (Indirect)
   "Would you please eat your peas?" (Indirect)

2. Negotiations, positive or negative, as in . . .

   "If you'll eat your peas, I'll let you have some ice cream."
   "If you don't eat your peas, you're going straight to your room."

When they're angry, Harriet and John set their commands and negotiations and requests to the tune of English hostility, with lots of extra emphatic stresses on words and parts of words. And they aren't careful to make what they want *clear*, relying on vague utterances like "You settle down!" and "You straighten up!"

Three-part messages would help. They don't guarantee agreement from children; of course not. Human beings want to do things *their* way, and children are no exception. But three-part messages are a way to get past some of the *automatic* negative reaction children (and other adults) have to being told what to do. The less out of control the situation is, the more helpful this technique will be.

The three-part message started out as a classic pattern called "the I-message" (as in "I feel embarrassed when you scream in the grocery store"). Dr. Thomas Gordon expanded this by adding one more piece to it. Here's the final pattern:

"When you [X], I feel [Y], because [Z]."
      1   2   3

- Part 1 contains the *specific* item of behavior that the speaker wants changed; starting with "When you" puts the focus squarely on that item.

- Part 2 states the emotion the speaker *feels* about the item of behavior.

- Part 3 states the real-world consequences of the behavior that justify the request.

All three parts should be concrete and verifiable in the real world; ideally, none of them will include anything that a reasonable person would argue about. Look at the following examples.

TYPICAL COMPLAINT AND COMMAND

"I can't beLIEVE you forgot to water the tomato plants aGAIN! You KNOW you're supposed to water them! If YOU don't STOP skipping all your chores and goofing OFF, you are going to be one VEry SORry CHILD!"

Or, stated even more vaguely,

"YOU had BETTER STOP behaving like you could just deCIDE for yourSELF what you have to do around here, or YOU are going to be SORry!"

Now compare these typical examples with a three-part message that you could use in exactly the same situation.

THREE-PART MESSAGE

"When you don't water the tomato plants, I feel angry, because plants die if they're not watered."

Part 1, "When you don't water the tomato plants," is absolutely concrete and verifiable—all you have to do is look at the plants to see that it's true. It states the one specific item of behavior that the speaker wants changed, and it contains no extra baggage. No moral judgments. No embellishments. Part 2, "I feel angry," is verifiable because the speaker's body language backs it up and it's appropriate to the situation. Part 3, "Because plants die if they're not watered," is a simple statement of fact; you can verify it any time by leaving a plant unwatered and watching what happens. Reasonable people would find nothing here to argue about.

Once in a while someone in a seminar tells me (or a reader writes) that it's a serious mistake to say "I feel angry" to a child. I don't think so. Children know perfectly well that real people in the real world get mad, and they know that the anger is often directed at kids. Pretending that that's not true doesn't fool children, because the adult's body language will always betray the truth. There's nothing wrong with an adult saying "I feel angry."

I do recognize the limitations of the three-part message when used with children. Children are likely not to *be* reasonable people when you cross them, and they will try arguing when no adult would even think about it. Little Linda from Scenario Three would jump right in and try to argue that plants *don't* die when they're not watered. That makes the technique no less useful in adult–child communication. Even when the person spoken to is a tiny child, using the three-part message offers two substantial benefits:

1. It provides the child with a valuable *model* for requesting a change in behavior.

2. It makes it easier for the furious adult to keep from saying things that will only make the situation worse.

When adults are really angry with kids and they know their anger is justified, it's hard for them not to say hurtful or exaggerated things they'll regret later. Having the three-part message available as a pattern in such situations makes natural mistakes of that kind much less likely.

Following the Pattern

I want to stress that it's important to follow the three-part message pattern as closely as possible because it's so easy to ruin the message by making small changes. Changes that seem completely trivial can have very bad results. Especially when, as is so often the case in disagreements between adults and children, you're already angry. Anger makes us careless with our words. Resist the temptation to tinker with the pattern; it works, just the way it is.

Here are five examples of attempted three-part messages that *won't* work, with explanations.

1. "When you act the way you do, I feel _____"

It makes no difference how the rest of the message goes; this is a failure. "When you act the way you do" gives children almost *no* information about what item of their behavior you want them to change. You may be convinced that your child *does* know what you mean by this utterance, but much of the time you're wrong: All the child knows is that he or she is in trouble. If you yourself don't know what specific item of behavior you object to, how can you expect the child to know?

2. "When you act like some kind of animal, I feel _____"

Again, there's no point in going on. "When you act like some kind of animal" is a moral judgment and an accusation. It's just as vague as "when you act the way you do" or "when you do the things you do." And it contains additional hostile messages that don't belong there.

3. "When you forget to water the tomato plants, you make me angry, because plants die if they're not watered."

Here the problem is that "you make me angry" has been used instead of "I feel angry." For one thing, "you make me angry" is a separate complaint; a successful three-part message should ask for a change in *only one* item of behavior. More importantly, "you make me angry" presupposes that the child has the power to determine what emotion you feel. If that's true, it would be wise to keep it to yourself. Variations like "you make me angry" and "it drives me crazy" are tempting, but they should be avoided. Just use "I feel" and name the emotion.

4. "When you forget my birthday, I feel sad, because it means you don't love me."

Parts 1 and 2 are fine, but Part 3 is a failure. There's no way to verify "you don't love me" in the real world. It's not a consequence of the behavior you're objecting to; it's just one speaker's opinion. Remember: The goal is for all three parts of your message to be things that no reasonable person could argue about. "It means you don't love me" *begs* for an argument.

5. "When you don't make your bed, I feel angry, because I always had to make *my* bed."

Messages like this one are the reason I recommend that people write down what they're going to say in advance, if they have time. You don't want to hear this sentence coming out of your mouth. If you see it written down, you'll know that *before* you say it. The most predictable response to sentence 5, and one that's justified, is, "What does that have to do with anything?" "Because I always had to" do something is the exact adult equivalent of "Because all the other kids" have or do something, and it's just as irrelevant.

Another good reason for writing down the three-part message before you say it is that you'll find out in advance whether you can fill all three parts. If you can't—if you don't know what item of behavior you want changed, or how you feel about that behavior, or what its undesirable real world consequences are—maybe you should reconsider. Maybe it's not something you should be complaining about.

I know only two possible changes in the three-part message pattern that may be useful. One is making it more neutral by taking out the *personal* language, when that's appropriate. For example, you might make this change if you need to complain for somebody *else*. Suppose you're a police officer who's been called in because a teenage band, practicing in a garage, is playing too loud. In a situation like that, "I feel angry" isn't the best choice, no matter how the officer feels about loud amateur rock music. Instead, the message should be something like this:

"When you play so loud that you can be heard a block away, people feel angry, because they can't go to sleep and they have to get up and go to work in the morning."

Or, even *less* personally,

"When music is played so loud that it can be heard a block away, people feel angry, because they can't go to sleep and they have to get up and go to work in the morning."

Any time you're dealing with a youngster you know will react very defensively or angrily to a request for changed behavior, this change is worth considering. It's easier for kids to agree with a complaint framed as a statement about a general or hypothetical situation than one that's openly aimed at them personally. *Of course* this is a fiction; the children know that the message is really meant for them. But this wording is like offering the illusion of choice — it carries a metamessage that says roughly:

"I realize that being told what to do puts you in a bind. You feel like you're obligated to resist because you'd lose face if you just agreed. I'm making an effort not to put you in that awkward position."

People sometimes think that losing face is an idea that applies only to other cultures — the Japanese, for instance. This is false. For children, who are already in a "one down" position with adults, *avoiding loss of face is usually far more important than the content of the complaint.*

When I was a teenager my parents gave me an eleven o'clock curfew on weekends, even though my friends were allowed to stay out much later. I saw this as intolerably unjust. So, no matter how bored I was—no matter how much I really wanted to go home—I always stayed out late enough on weekends to be *certain* I wouldn't make it home till five minutes after eleven. It wasn't that I wanted to stay out; it was a matter of saving face. Many youngsters react negatively to requests for behavior changes even when they have no objection to the change at all. *Their reaction is to the fact that they're being told what to do.* A three-part message helps you get past that knee-jerk negative so that the child can *hear* what you're saying and give it fair consideration. Taking the personal words out of the message can sometimes make that even easier.

The other permissible change is filling Part 3 with a related fact that no reasonable person would argue about, when no real-world consequence is available. For example: "When you say '[a four-letter word],' I feel distressed, because '[four-letter word]' is something only grownups are allowed to say."

Now, what if you find that you *can't* construct a three-part message? What if one of the three parts is missing and you just can't find a way to fill that slot?

Remember the example on page 74 that started with "When you forget my birthday?" The reason it can't be completed is because it has no verifiable real-world consequence (or related real-world fact that would be appropriate.) That's going to happen sometimes. There will be times when you want to state your negative feelings about something a child does, but you really *can't* turn them into a three-part message. That doesn't mean that you can't say what you feel. "When you forget my birthday, I feel sad" is a valid statement and it's probably something that the child needs to hear. Just remember that it doesn't qualify as a three-part message.

The difference between a simple statement of feelings and a three-part message is in the communication *goals*. The goal of a three-part message isn't to express the speaker's feelings or to inform the listener. It's to *bring about a change in the listener's behavior.* "When you keep clicking your ballpoint pen like that, I feel angry" is a fine way to express your feelings and educate the child about them; there's nothing wrong with it. But it's not as likely to cause the child to stop clicking the ballpoint pen as a three-part message—which offers a concrete real-world consequence as a reason for the request—is.

Praise and Three-Part Messages

The three-part message pattern, designed for making complaints about behavior and requesting changes, is also extremely useful for messages of *praise.* Small children love praise and can absorb huge amounts of it without blinking. But youngsters older than nine or ten are often (like most adults) *suspicious* about praise; they think, "What's the catch? What does this person <u>want</u> from <u>me</u>?" The three-part message gets around this reaction just as it gets around the reaction to complaints, by stating exactly what item of behavior deserves praise, how the speaker feels about that, and what real world fact justifies the compliment. Ideally, again, no part of the message is anything a reasonable person could argue about, as in these examples:

> "When you get an A in math, I feel proud, because your teacher told me she almost never gives A's in math."

> "When you clean up the kitchen after your snack, I feel pleased, because I can start dinner right away when I get home from work."

> "When you do your work on time, I feel pleased, because I can't start my own work until I have yours."

For unusually touchy kids, you can do an impersonal version, like this:

> "When the filing is turned in on time, people feel pleased, because they can't start their own work until they have all the files."

Body Language and Three-Part Messages

Adults need to be extremely careful about the body language they use with their three-part messages. There's nothing special about the words in these messages that makes them an exception to the English rules about body language. Like any other words, they'll be canceled by body language that conflicts with them. Compare these two messages:

MESSAGE A

> "When you bring the car home with an empty tank, I feel distressed, because I can't drive it to work the next day without having to stop at the gas station."

MESSAGE B

> "When you bring the CAR home with an empty TANK, I feel DISTRESSED, because I can't drive it to WORK the next day without having to STOP at the GAS station!"

The words in the two messages are identical. But they carry very different metamessages. A's metamessage just says that the utterance is asking for a change in behavior; it's a *neutral* utterance. B is definitely not neutral. B is at least "and I am really FURIOUS with you about this!" and maybe "and I think you're a rotten CREEP of a KID!" as well. *How* negative it is depends entirely on the body language that goes *with* its words.

In the same way, when a three-part praise message is spoken in a hostile voice with a smirk on the speaker's face, it won't be *understood* as praise. The negative body language cancels the words' emotional content and turns them into sarcasm.

Now let's stop and apply this information to Scenario Three.

Another Look at Scenario Three

John and Harriet Lassiter ask their children to change their behavior — or try to ask them to! — several times during this scenario. Here are the relevant lines.

John: "You settle <u>down</u>, or you're getting a <u>spanking</u>!"

"I can carry you <u>out</u> of here, and when I get you out to the <u>car</u> I'll blister your sassy little <u>tail</u>!"

"Linda Charlotte Lassiter _____ "

Harriet: "I want you to straighten up, <u>right</u> now! I am disgusted by your behavior, and I want it to <u>stop</u>."

"<u>Don't</u> make me have to tell you <u>again</u>, young lady!"

Both Lassiters also send many change-your-behavior messages with body language — by grabbing the children, holding them, dragging them away, and so on — as well as in the things they say to one another, such as: "I'm not going to talk to them again until they're <u>thirty</u>."

Nobody could say the Lassiters aren't trying hard to persuade their kids to behave differently. Obviously they have the best of intentions. They aren't the kinds of parents you see sometimes, who seem to feel that no rules apply to *their* offspring, no matter how unpleasant that is for other people around them. But all the Lassiter parents' sincere efforts are wasted. Their language — both words and body language — serves very well as an outlet for their emotions, and as a kind of punishment. But it does nothing at all to improve their children's rotten behavior.

The first problem is the vagueness of their language. Kids who are out of control need to hear *exactly* what you want from them, not "settle down" or "straighten up." (Unless, of course, "settle down" or "straighten up" are family code for use in public, with the precise meaning specified in private.) It's very common for clients who consult me about talking to their children to tell me that the kids "most certainly *do* know!" what the adults are angry about. But when I ask the youngsters why they think their parents are angry, without the adults present, they say things like these:

"It's because they <u>hate</u> me, <u>that's</u> all."

"It's because I'm no good."

"It's because I can't do <u>anything</u> right, <u>ever</u>!"

"It's just because they're <u>mean</u>."

"It's because I'm stupid."

And, once in a while . . .

"They <u>say</u> it's because I get C's in school, but that's just an excuse. It's <u>really</u> because they <u>hate</u> me."

✦ When requests for changed behavior are buried in metamessages of anger and disgust, it's the emotional messages that are heard and believed and remembered.

If the Lassiters would rather ask for change by using commands (either direct or indirect), they'd be wise to make those commands *specific* and to say them without the extra stresses that signal hostility in English. They need to say things like "Keep your voice down and don't yell" and "Don't run around the table" and "Don't talk when someone else is talking, please" instead of "Settle down!" and "Straighten up!"

Their second serious error is letting their eight-year-old distract them with unrelated arguments. When John tells Linda to settle down or he'll spank her, she distracts him by starting an argument about whether he can spank her in public—and he takes her up on it. When Harriet is setting the stage for the command, "You have to be good in public to set an example for your brothers and sisters," she lets Linda distract her with a silly argument about playing with Kathleen's Barbie dolls. Both parents need to recognize this tactic of Linda's and learn not to fall into the trap. For example:

Harriet: "You have to be good, because your little sister and brother look up to you and copy your behavior."

Linda: "Kath<u>leen</u> doesn't look up to me! <u>She</u> won't even let me play with her <u>Bar</u>bies!"

Harriet: "You have to be good. Kathleen and Tommy do what they see <u>you</u> do."

Linda: "Mommy, I said Kathleen won't let me play with her Barbies! <u>You</u> always say we have to <u>share</u>."

Harriet: "And I say that you have to set a good example for your brother and sister, because you are the oldest."

That is: Harriet should stick to her topic—that Linda must set a good example for the younger children—and she must firmly ignore the child's attempts to lead her off on other subjects. If that means repeating herself half a dozen times, that's all right. The point is to demonstrate to Linda that Harriet *will not* fall for this trick any more, and that trying to force her to is going to be boring. Boredom is one thing that today's kids *are* afraid of.

Harriet also needs to remember that she's *right* about the younger children copying what they see Linda do. That means that—unless something is done to prevent it—Kathleen and Tommy will learn from Linda how to drive grownups frantic with insolence and distraction. Every time she and Linda get involved in a language interaction, the two younger children are watching and learning.

The Lassiter children appear to be completely out of control. That can't be fixed by one or two episodes of better communication. But it's time to *start*. The longer John and Harriett put it off, the more the children's bad linguistic habits will be set in concrete. Let's take a look at two examples that show what this beginning might be like.

1.

John: "When you yell and scream in public, kids, I feel angry, because the other people stare at us."

Linda: "<u>I</u> don't care! I'll just stare <u>back</u> at them and make <u>them</u> feel stupid!"

John: "I think you do care, Linda. Otherwise, you wouldn't feel stupid when you see them staring at you."

Linda: "It's not <u>polite</u> for them to stare at me!"

John: "That's right; it's not. And it's not polite for you to yell in the restaurant. Please don't do it."

Kathleen: "Daddy, can we yell and scream at home?"

John: "Sometimes. You just ask Linda; she'll always be able to tell you whether it's okay."

Linda: "Yeah, Kath! You just ask _me_!"

2.

Harriet: "Linda, when you say rude things to your father in front of Kathleen and Tommy, I feel sad, because little kids copy what they see big kids do."

Linda: "Kath_leen_ doesn't copy me!"

Kathleen: "I do _too_!"

Harriet: "Why, honey? Why do you copy your sister?"

Kathleen: "'Cause she's _big_!"

Harriet: "And Tommy copies you and Linda _both_, right?"

Kathleen: "Right!"

Tommy: "_Tommy_ do it!"

Harriet: "Notice, Linda . . . they think that when they see you do something—or _hear_ you do something—that means it's okay. Can you handle that? Can you be more careful, so they can learn?"

Linda: "I guess so."

Harriet: "Thank you, dear. Now . . . what was it that you wanted to tell me a minute ago?"

The Lassiters won't find this easy to do. It takes planning and patience. It means they have to think before they speak and carefully consider the possible consequences of what they say. It means they have to resist the temptation to lash out at kids who've grown so wild that they can only be controlled by physical force, and that's hard. But they need to remember these four important points:

1. Children learn their language behavior by observing the adults around them and the other models (such as television) that adults provide for them. *It's not the kids' fault if those models are bad ones.*

2. When kids are small, adults can control them by force just because the adults are bigger and stronger — but that's not a permanent condition. If they're still out of control when their size and strength begins to be equal to that of an adult, the situation will be hopeless.

3. The consequences of throwing up your hands and saying "It's too much <u>trouble</u>! I don't have <u>time</u>!" aren't confined to the present. They aren't just the embarrassment and expense of having to leave restaurants after you've already ordered. Down the road, when the children are adults with no idea how to get along in this world, or how to teach <u>their</u> children (your grandchildren!) to get along, the consequences for you as well as for them will be much more serious.

✦ For both adults and children, letting the kind of chaos shown in Scenario Three go on is literally dangerous to their health. For this reason, as well as to give themselves a chance for a serene future, *it's in the adults' own self-interest to make the effort to change things.* If they're not motivated to do it for the children's sake — maybe because they feel sure that schools and society will do it in their place — they should do it for what's in it for *them.* They'll be repaid for their investment of time and energy many times over.

One More Dialogue

I want to ask you now to consider one more dialogue. All of the problems we've looked at up to this point have been fairly minor ones. Annoying, distressing, embarrassing, perhaps, but fairly minor. I want to show you how a technique like the three-part message can help when you're dealing with something more serious.

The speakers in the following dialogue are a parent and a seventeen-year-old boy who has picked up some ugly and dangerous ideas.

DIALOGUE 12

Adult: "According to Marianne, you <u>hit</u> her last night."

Teen: "She ratted on me, huh? Well . . . she'll be sorry."

Adult: "You mean it's true? You really <u>hit</u> <u>her</u>?"

Teen: (*Shrugs.*) "It's cool. She was asking for it."

Adult: "You mean to tell me that you think it was OKAY TO HIT HER?"

Teen: "Hey, girls don't have any respect for you if you let 'em get away with stuff!"

Adult: "I cannot beLIEVE what I'm HEARING here! You HIT your girlfriend . . . to make her RESPECT YOU? HOW could you possibly DO that? How can you possibly SAY such terrible things? When you act like that, it makes me SICK, don't you KNOW THAT?"

Teen: "It's got nothing to DO with you!"

Adult: "It has EVERYthing to do with me!"

Teen: "Oh, yeah? Listen — I'm seven<u>teen</u>. I'm not a baby! And you can't TREAT me like a baby!"

Adult: "I am NOT treating you like a baby!"

Teen: "Yes, you ARE! You're trying to lay a lot of stuff on me that's just stuff YOU believe in! It's not right just because YOU say it, you know!"

Here we have an adult facing real trouble. The research on domestic violence in the United States today is very clear:

✦ Sane adult males who hit women share a set of negative attitudes *about* women that make it possible for them to justify their behavior to themselves.

That set of attitudes has been found in American boys as young as six or seven. The earlier the problem is caught and addressed, the better the chances are of convincing the abuser that hitting another person is *never* justified unless the abuser is literally in physical danger and can't escape it in any other way—a very rare set of circumstances.

When the adult in the dialogue lets the focus of attention shift from the boy's treatment of his girlfriend to the adult's treatment of *him*, a grave error has been made. If ever there was a place for a three-part message, this is it.

DIALOGUE 12 REVISITED

Adult: "According to Marianne, you <u>hit</u> her last night."

Teen: "She ratted on me, huh? Well . . . she'll be sorry."

Adult: "You mean it's true? You really <u>hit</u> her?"

Teen: (*Shrugs.*) "She was asking for it."

Adult: "You mean to tell me that you think it was OKAY TO HIT HER?"

Teen: "Hey, girls don't have any respect for you if you let 'em get away with stuff!"

Adult: "Tom, when I hear you say it's okay to hit a woman, I feel sick, because violence is one of the most serious problems this country faces today."

Every attempt this boy makes to distract the adult from the issue should be met with another message of the same kind, ending with a "because" statement that is neither an emotional cry nor a moral judgment but a *cold hard fact,* as in these examples:

- "When I hear you say that men have to hit women to maintain their respect, I feel sick, because the majority of men who hit their female partners also hit their children."

- "When I hear you claim that hitting women is acceptable if they 'asked' for it, I feel <u>very</u> sad, because the children of men who physically abuse their wives tend to grow up and follow their example."

• "When I hear you say, '[whatever the child is saying, quoted exactly as it was stated],' I feel angry, because the cost of domestic violence in the United States last year was more than eighty billion dollars that could have been spent on roads and education and health care."

The focus of the interaction, when an adult faces a child who is championing violence (or any other horror) has to be kept on the *behavior.* However intense the adult's feelings are, the language should be kept as unemotional and free of melodramatic pronouncements as possible. When an interaction like the one in the dialogue turns into an emotional extravaganza, it may make the adult feel better, but it doesn't accomplish anything useful. A communication breakdown is only going to make a terrible situation worse.

It's hard, when you're genuinely shocked or sickened by a child's behavior, to talk *without* getting carried away. Having the three-part message as a pattern to fall back on at such times can keep the communication lines open in spite of the revulsion you're feeling, and it's critically important to do that. Probably the most important time of all to keep communication going is when your gut feeling is that you don't care whether you *ever* talk to the child again. In situations like that, rely on the three-part message to get you through it.

Talking to the Cyberchild

In talking to the cyberchild, you may need three-part messages like these:

"When you use technical computer terms, I feel baffled, because conversation is difficult unless everybody who's talking knows the meanings of the words being used."

"When you say, 'I can't beLIEVE you don't know what a SERial PORT is!', I feel surprised, because many people don't know anything at all about serial ports."

"When you say, 'How long can it TAKE to answer ONE SIM-PLE QUEStion?', I feel irritated, because people often can't do things as fast as computers can."

"When you say you're going to have your nose pierced, I feel distressed, because most people don't pierce anything but their ears."

You'll notice that all of these messages end with a related and non-controversial real-world *fact* instead of a *consequence*. That satisfies two of the requirements for Part 3: that it be objective, not judgmental, and that it be something reasonable people wouldn't argue about. Filling Part 3 with a consequence is better, always. But the consequence must be realistic. The problem with messages such as "When you say you're going to have your nose pierced, I feel distressed, because when kids get their noses pierced their ears fall off" is that they aren't *true*.

———————— ✦ ————————

CHAPTER 4

Don't you feel any remorse at <u>all</u>?

Using the Satir Modes

———————— Scenario Four ————————

The police officer stared at the two boys sitting across the table from him, and they stared back; the blankness in their eyes turned his stomach. He reminded himself that these were *children,* and went on talking.

"I don't think you under<u>stand</u>," he said grimly. "We had to take the Nelson boy to the eMERgency room after you two worked him over. Do you understand THAT?"

"Yeah. <u>We</u> understand," said twelve-year-old Sean Philips. His brother Kevin was two years older, but Sean seemed to be the one in charge. "So <u>what</u>?"

That did it. It was the eighth or ninth smart crack in a row; it was too much for the officer.

"So WHAT?" he demanded. "What do you <u>mean</u>, 'so what'? So, this is SERious! You guys really HURT him! If you'd hit him a couple <u>more</u> times, he'd have LOST that eye! DON'T you even CARE?"

"Nope."

"How about you?" Bill Markson turned his head toward the other boy. "Do YOU CARE?"

Kevin's lips twitched. "<u>Hey</u>, man," he said, "<u>we</u> just did what we <u>had</u> to do, out there, Sean and me! YOU don't push any of OUR buttons!"

Bill closed his eyes and took a deep breath, thinking it over. *They're kids,* he told himself. *That means teddy bears. That means proms and pompoms. That means . . .* But it was no use. He kept seeing the bruised and bloody face of the other boy, the one these two had beaten up because they wanted his jacket and he didn't want to give it to them.

He opened his eyes and stood up with his hands on his hips. "I'm THROUGH talking to you!" he announced. When both boys began to clap silently, he ignored it. "Your FOLKS are out there," he told them. "Let's get THEM in here to talk to you!"

Evelyn Philips stared at her boys, too, and then at her husband, and then back at the boys. She couldn't believe this was happening. "Sean . . . Kevin . . . He says you beat up Kenneth Nelson so badly that they had to take him to the hospital. He says it was because you wanted Kenny's jacket. Surely that can't be TRUE!"

"Yeah," Sean answered. "It's true."

"But how could you POSSibly DO such a horrible thing?" she gasped. "What's the MATTER with you boys—have you LOST your MINDS?"

"It's no big deal, Mom," Sean said calmly. "Don't make a federal case out of it. Okay?"

"Yeah, Mom," Kevin put in. "Nelson's not gonna die or anything."

Their father spoke then. He was clutching the edge of the table so tightly that his knuckles were white.

"YOU little creeps!" he spat. "YOU little _____"

"Now, DAvid _____"

"STAY OUT of this, Evelyn! I'M TALKing to these animals here! YOU HEAR ME, SEAN? KEVIN? I'M TALKING to you, and I say you're both ANImals! YOU'RE not even HUman!"

"So take us to the zoo," said Sean, leaning back in the wooden chair till it teetered on its back legs.

Beside him, Kevin snickered, "Good line, Sean-o!" He punched Sean once in the ribs, softly.

"The zoo is too damn GOOD for YOU, buddy!" their father shouted. "MONsters is what you are, YOU HEAR ME? MONsters!"

Evelyn turned to the boys, tears in her eyes. "Don't listen to him!" she said frantically. "He's sick about this . . . we're both sick about it . . . we don't understand. He doesn't mean the things he's saying!"

The boys shrugged.

"Hey, Mom," Sean said, "don't sweat it! It doesn't matter to Kevin and me. Animals . . . monsters . . . Whatever. We don't care."

And that's the truth, thought the watching officer. They <u>don't</u> care. Not about anything in this world but themselves. God help their parents, he thought. *And God help us all.*

--------------------------- ✦ ---------------------------

What's Going On Here?

This scenario is ugly. And it's not rare; it happens every day. Every day children are caught committing violent crimes. The adults who have to deal with that and who try to talk to them draw one conclusion: *These kids don't care. They <u>literally</u> don't care. They feel absolutely no remorse for what they've done.*

There *are* people who have no conscience, who can hurt others without a flicker of concern. They feel no guilt, no matter what they do; their only regret in a situation like the one in Scenario Four is regret that they've been caught. These people are called *sociopaths* (or *psychopaths*), and they are very sick individuals. They lack human feeling in exactly the same way someone else might lack an arm or a leg. This is an illness, as serious as cancer and not nearly as well understood. Nobody knows what—if anything—can be done to cure such people; so far, our society deals with them by locking them up.

If the boys in the scenario were sociopaths, or even hardened criminals, I wouldn't try to discuss them here. Discussions of such children belong in the technical books written for professionals in mental health and criminal justice. But Sean and Kevin are normal ordinary kids, and this criminal incident is their first. They've been in trouble a few times, at school and at home, for fighting with other kids and for insolence—but they've never before done anything serious. Since that's true, we can concentrate here on the communication problem shown in the scenario: How do well-intentioned and law-abiding adults—adults who are trying to do the right thing and who *believe* in doing the right thing—talk to children who seem to feel only contempt for the standards of society? When adults have good reason to believe that a normal human child is somewhere behind the hateful monster facade, what can they say that will get them past the mask?

The temptation to say it's hopeless is very strong. And there's a worse temptation (the one the father gave in to in the scenario) in which you refuse even to try, because you are so repulsed by the children that all you want to do is drum them out of the human race.

These reactions are understandable, especially when the crime is violent. But we can't afford them. We've already run out of money just for the forced exiling of *adults* who won't follow society's rules. Let's set these temptations aside for now and consider exactly what's going on in language interactions like the one above. Two points need special emphasis:

- It's the *children* who are in control of the situation in Scenario Four, not the adults. The children are playing a game and using the adults as their pawns.

- Almost everything the adults say or do is *a reaction to the language the children use.*

We all know, as adults, that this isn't how it's supposed to be. If we talked to Officer Markson, or to Mr. and Mrs. Philips, we'd quickly learn that they know that too. They know that losing their tempers, crying, and using verbal violence with the boys was neither appropriate nor useful. *But,* they would tell us, the boys infuriated and repelled them so much that they just plain could not *help* behaving as they did!

The key here—since we know Sean and Kevin aren't monsters—is that what *triggered* the adults' loss of control was the boys' language. Bad as the violence was, the adults do know that kids sometimes do awful things for reasons other than inherent wickedness—just to try them out, just to prove how "cool" or tough they are, just to impress their peers. That knowledge should have meant patience and compassion, at least for a while. But everything went to pieces in the scenario very quickly. The question is, then, is there something that could be done, short of gagging and handcuffing the boys, to keep things from going downhill so fast? Are there systematic linguistic strategies the adults could use instead of just reacting?

The answer, I'm glad to say, is yes. Whether you're trying to communicate with youngsters in a grave situation involving criminal acts, or just facing garden-variety insolence, the technique we're about to discuss will help.

I realize that your final goal is to change the *child*. But that process is long and difficult at best. Often it requires either the lessons that come only from real-life experiences over years, or the help of experts, or both. What you have to do *first* is establish an atmosphere where communication can happen. To do that—so that you have a *chance* to do something more—you have to start by changing the language. This is something that you can do yourself, without any outside experts, using the tools you're already equipped with: your native language competence, your adult knowledge of the real world, and your own common sense. It isn't easy when you have to deal with youngsters like Kevin and Sean, but it's not impossible.

What to Do About It—
Using the Satir Modes

No one is surprised to hear that the language behavior of people under stress—whatever their age—is different from that of people who are relaxed and comfortable. We all know that people who are upset talk differently; we've all seen tantrums and fretting and many other variations. But we don't have to stop at just calling such communication "emotional" or "tense"; we can be more specific than that.

Recognizing the Satir Modes

During her long career as a family therapist, Dr. Virginia Satir discovered that the language behavior of people under stress falls into one of five patterns: *Blaming, Placating, Computing, Distracting,* and *Leveling.* Suppose five teenagers have been waiting for job interviews that were supposed to start at nine o'clock sharp; suppose it's now ten and nobody has been called in yet. Here are some typical things they might say, one from each of the Satir Modes.

BLAMING

"Hey, if <u>they</u> think I'M gonna sit around here all morning, they're <u>wrong</u>! They made a GREAT BIG DEAL out of how WE had to be here right on TIME, and now THEY'RE a whole hour LATE! JUST because they've got a couple of crummy JOBS to give out . . . they think they OWN us or something! SHEEESH!"

PLACATING

"I <u>bet</u> I wrote down the wrong <u>time</u> for this interview . . . I didn't <u>mean</u> to, I mean, I was TRYing to be careful! But like, I can't beLIEVE they wouldn't have called ANYbody in if we were REALLY supposed to be here at NINE! NOT that anybody's gonna give ME a job ANYway . . . they NEVer DO . . ."

COMPUTING

"There's gotta be a good reason why the interviews haven't started yet; otherwise, somebody would have said something. Leaving now would be ridiculous. Waiting around is a bummer, though."

DISTRACTING

"I'm SURE they have a good REASon for all this waiting. They've GOTTA have! Not that <u>I'M</u> any expert on stuff like this, but PEOPle don't just keep you WAITing a whole hour for NOTHing, DO THEY? I mean, I'm REALLY getting SICK of this! THIS is how people TREAT kids, you KNOW what I MEAN? People don't think they have to be polite to anybody under twenty."

LEVELING

"They said to be here at nine, and I was; now it's ten o'clock. I wish they'd hurry up and start. I'm not going to wait much longer."

You will have recognized these patterns right away (though you may not have known their names). We all use them, or we hear other people use them; they're part of our internal grammar. Here's a list of their identifying characteristics.

BLAMING

Lots of very personal "I/me/you/this" language.

Extra stresses (emphasis) on words and parts of words.

Frequent use of words like "always," "everybody," "never."

A surface impression of anger and hostility.

PLACATING

Lots of very personal "I/me/you/this" language.

Extra stresses on words and parts of words.

A surface impression of apology and a desperate desire to please.

COMPUTING

Very *little* personal language; lots of generics and abstractions.

No extra stresses on words and parts of words.

A surface impression of control and reasonableness.

DISTRACTING

Distracting is cycling through the other modes . . . a sentence or two of Blaming, a sentence of Placating, a little Computing . . . The surface impression is frantic, with the speaker seeming not to know *what* to say, but unable to stop talking.

LEVELING

Leveling is what's left over. When language behavior under stress isn't one of the other four Satir Modes, it will be Leveling.

The Satir Modes are linguistic strategies for dealing with stressful situations and conflict. They're learned by observation and are linked to particular roles and situations. People have strong preferences among these patterns and rely heavily on the ones they believe work best for them. Many people rely on Blaming to deal with conflict at home and always use Placating in tense situations elsewhere, or vice versa. Which Satir Modes children use and when they start using them will depend on what they observe in others in their language environment. The adults' role here is like their role for the language traffic rules: They need to provide children with good *models* for using the Satir Modes successfully. To do this, they only have to remember the metaprinciple:

✦ Anything you feed will grow.

All language interactions are interactive feedback loops. What we say in any language interaction is based on what we hear from the other speakers involved. What they say is based on what they hear from us. We set up communication loops, and what happens to them depends on whether we feed them or not. When you respond to Blaming with Blaming, you set up a Blaming loop that will keep on growing for as long as it's fed. The same thing is true for all the modes.

You will recognize a particular Satir Mode coming at you, almost automatically, if you're paying attention and on the alert for these patterns. Your next move is to ask yourself: *Do I want this to grow? Is this something I'd like to see continue and escalate?* If your answer is yes, you can get what you want by feeding the loop—by matching the other person's Satir Mode. Let's take a look at a few sample language loops for four of the Satir Modes—all but Distracting. (Because Distracting back at someone is panic feeding panic and will *always* guarantee a communication disaster, we can skip that one.)

Sample Dialogues

DIALOGUE 13: Blaming Back at Blaming

Child: "WHY do you ALways make me eat YUCKY stuff? YOU NEVer make anything I like! YOU'RE MEAN!"

Adult: "I am <u>not</u> mean! What you <u>like</u> has nothing to to <u>do</u> with it — you have to eat food that's <u>good</u> for you! Now <u>stop</u> com- <u>plaining</u>, and <u>eat</u> your lunch!"

Child: "I HATE you!"

Adult: "GO TO YOUR ROOM!"

✦ A Blaming loop always means a fight.

DIALOGUE 14: Placating Back at Placating

Child: "But I don't LIKE tomato soup! PLEASE don't make me eat it! You KNOW what will happen — I'LL get SICK!"

Adult: "I'M sorry, honey, but it's too <u>late</u> to fix anything else now. I'd be GLAD to if I <u>could</u>, but it's just not POSSible! Can't you just TRY? For ME?"

Child: "(*Long sigh.*) Well . . . If you WANT me to get sick . . . I GUESS I can . . ."

Adult: "Of COURSE I don't want you to get sick! I LOVE you!"

Child: "Then you won't make me EAT it, WILL you?"

Adult: "But honey, I just TOLD you _____"

(And so on. And on. And on.)

DIALOGUE 15: Computing Back at Computing

Child: "Grownups shouldn't yell at kids."

Adult: "Grownups don't yell at kids unless there's a good reason to."

Child: "Different people have different ideas about what's a good reason."

Adult: "That's right."

Child: "Grownups probably think eating stupid tomato soup is a big deal, so it's okay to yell."

Adult: "Kids may not understand that people have to eat what's served to them."

(And so on.)

✦ A Computing loop always means a *dignified* delay.

DIALOGUE 16: *Leveling Back at Leveling*

Child: "I hate tomato soup. I always have."

Adult: "I know you do. I don't like it much either. But we have to eat it anyway."

Child: "It's all there is?"

Adult: "Right."

Child: "Okay."

✦ A Leveling loop is the simple truth going in both directions.

Leveling loops aren't necessarily pleasant; it depends on what the simple truth *is*. Suppose one child asks another, "You don't like me, do you?" and the answer is, "No, I don't. I think you're nerdy, and I don't want to play with you." Suppose a homely child asks an adult, "Am I ugly?" and the answer is, "Yes, you are. You are a really ugly child." These are also Leveling loops.

In *theory*, the truth is always the ideal message. But in practice — in the real world — there are many times when it's inappropriate or dangerous, or both.

Responding to the Satir Modes

Most of the time, you aren't going to want a fight; much of the time, you won't want a delay, dignified or not. Lots of times, at least at the beginnings of conversations, you won't know whether you can risk a "truth loop." This means that you'll often need to respond to one Satir Mode with a *different* one. The question is, which one? How do you choose?

Suppose you've recognized a child's language as Placating. She's trying to get you to do one of her math problems for her, by pleading and begging. She's using her most pitiful little voice and her most dramatic Poor Little Baby face. You know you don't want to answer her with Distracting. Let's consider the other three choices.

Sample Dialogues

DIALOGUE 17: Blaming Response to a Placating Child

Child: "PLEASE do this problem for me? PLEASE? You KNOW it's too HARD for me . . . I'M just a LITTLE KID! YOU don't want me to get YELLED at, DO YOU?"

Adult: "OH, for heaven's SAKES, STOP WHINing! I certainly will NOT do your arithmetic problem for you!"

This is one way to do it. It lets the adult express legitimate annoyance. It transmits two messages: that the Placating isn't going to work and that the adult isn't going to do the problem. The most likely next line from the child is something like, "YOU don't LOVE me! WHAT am I going to DOOOO?" . . . which won't make the adult feel any more pleasant toward the youngster. Both adult and child will come out of this angry and resentful. The two primary markers of hostile speech in American Mainstream English are highly personal vocabulary and extra emphatic stresses on words and parts of words. Since those are typical of both Placating and Blaming, the two are always a bad combination. In any order, they create a *Hostility* Loop.

DIALOGUE 17 REVISITED: Leveling Response to a Placating Child

Child "PLEASE do this problem for me? PLEASE? You KNOW it's too HARD for me . . . I'M just a LITTLE KID! YOU don't want me to get YELLED at, DO YOU?"

Adult: "I don't want you to get yelled at, no, and I'll be glad to help you with the problem. But I won't do it <u>for</u> you."

This is better than Blaming. The adult hasn't said anything hostile and has offered to help—but has clearly said the child has to do the problem herself. What happens next will depend on many factors. The most important one is the child's past experience. Here's one way Dialogue 17 might continue:

Child: "YOU ALways treat me that way! YOU don't LOVE me! YOU'RE going to make me DO it all by mySELF, even if it IS too hard!"

Adult: "Yes. You have to do it yourself."

Child: "But you'll help me?"

Adult: "Sure. Show me what you're having trouble with."

The child has made one more valiant try. But when all she gets for it is more Leveling, she gives up and switches to Leveling herself—indicating that she's learned from previous experience that it's a waste of her time to go on Placating, at least with this adult. If her experience *hasn't* been like that, she may have reason to believe that if she just keeps on Placating long enough the adult will break down, perhaps with, "OH, GOOD GRIEF! All RIGHT, I'll DO it! But JUST THIS ONCE!" In that case, she won't stop so easily.

DIALOGUE 17 REVISITED: Computing Response to a Placating Child

Child: "PLEASE do this problem for me? PLEASE? You KNOW it's too HARD for me . . . I'M just a LITTLE KID! YOU don't want me to get YELLED at, DO YOU?"

Adult: "When grownups do children's homework for them, it's a mistake. Because then the children don't learn how to do it."

As was true with the Leveling response, the adult has said nothing hostile, but the message is that the child has to do the problem herself. Which may lead to this:

Child: "But I can't DO it! I'll get in trouble!"

Adult: "It's not okay for grownups to do kids' homework for them. It <u>is</u> okay for a grownup just to help."

Child: "Will you help me, please?"

Adult: "Sure."

The Leveling and Computing responses are obviously better than the Blaming one. Even if the Blaming adult ends by offering to help, it's hard for a youngster to learn — or an adult to teach — when they're both in a state of emotional turmoil. Choosing between Leveling and Computing is better; which of those two you choose will depend on the situation and the people involved. Because Computing is the most *neutral* choice, it's the better alternative when you aren't sure what to do.

The rules for responding to the Satir Modes are:

✦ RULE ONE: If what's coming at you from the other person is something you want to encourage, match that Satir Mode.

✦ RULE TWO: If you don't know what to do, use Computer Mode until you have a good reason to change.

Even if using Rule Two will create a Computing loop, the worst thing that can happen is a dignified delay. That's better than Blaming or Placating and ending up in a fight. It's also better than Leveling and having to be sorry later because the truth turned out to be inappropriate or harmful or both.

What we see in Scenario Four is three adults who aren't making any *deliberate* Satir Mode choices at all. They're simply *reacting* to the language they hear from the two boys and from one another, with no thought for the consequences and no underlying communication strategy.

Listen to the language coming at you; you will recognize the Satir Mode you hear automatically. Remember the consequences of setting up each type of Satir Mode loop. Ask yourself: "Is this a loop I want to help establish and maintain? Do I want this kind of language behavior to grow?" If so, match the mode; if not, go to Computer Mode until you have a reason to change.

Body Language and the Satir Modes

Remember that for English more than 90 percent of all emotional information, and at least 65 percent of *all* information, is carried by the body language used, not by the words. Remember that body language can always cancel out words, but not vice versa. This means that *the only way you can be sure which Satir Mode you're hearing or using is through body language.* Some words turn up oftener in one mode than in another, but any word whatsoever can be used in any Satir Mode. The body language — especially the tone and intonation of the voice — is always the critical deciding factor. Compare these two sentences, from adults speaking to children:

1. "If you want to be on the team, you'll have to get to practice on time."

2. "If you want to be on the TEAM, YOU'LL have to get to PRACtice on TIME!"

The words are exactly the same in both sentences. But sentence 1 is just a statement of the information the child needs to have in order to be on the team. It's what an adult would say if a child had asked, "What do I have to do if I want to be on the soccer team?" Sentence 2 is very different: it's an *accusation.* It implies that the child has already come late to practice and that the adult is angry about that. Sentence 1 is Leveling; sentence 2 is Blaming. *The only reason the two sentences mean different things is because they're set to different tunes; only the body language is different.*

One thing you can do to avoid the negative meaning that goes with the word "if" is substitute "suppose," as I've frequently done in this book. Say, "Suppose you want to be on the team. Then you'll have to get to practice on time." This carries the *positive* "if" message for you. (I learned this from Bounlieng Chomphosy, whose native Lao language uses it for the same purpose.)

Here are some typical body language characteristics for each of the Satir Modes:

BLAMING

Frowning; scowling; sneering; tight lips and narrowed eyes; jabbing, pointing, and punching gestures; looming over people; very loud speech, or icy words through clenched teeth; extra emphatic stresses on words and parts of words. That is: *threatening* body language.

PLACATING

Wiggling and fidgeting; blinking eyelids; obviously phony smiles; leaning on other people; whiny or breathless tone of voice; extra emphatic stresses on words and parts of words. Satir summarized Placating body language, comparing it to that of a cocker spaniel puppy — desperate to please.

COMPUTING

As little body language as can possibly be used; few or no gestures; a carefully neutral facial expression and posture; a calm, sometimes almost monotonous intonation.

DISTRACTING

The body language in Distracting will shift from mode to mode right along with the words.

LEVELING

The most important characteristic is the absence of extra emphatic stresses on words and parts of words. The body language will *match* the words and the feelings of the speaker. That means that when children using Blaming say, "I'M going to RUN away from HOME!", they may only be saying that to threaten the adult listener. But when children using Leveling say the same words *without those extra emphatic stresses,* it's probable that they do intend to run away.

Now let's take a look at how the Satir Mode technique can be helpful in situations that are not as grim as the one in Scenario Four.

Sample Dialogues

DIALOGUE 18 (with a fourteen-year-old boy)

Adult: "<u>You</u> haven't done the <u>dishes</u>!"

Teen: "That's <u>right</u>, I <u>haven</u>'t."

Adult: "Well, would you get them <u>done</u>, <u>please</u>?"

Teen: "No."

Adult: "<u>No</u>? What do you <u>mean</u>, no?

Teen: "What I <u>mean</u> is, I'm <u>not</u> <u>going</u> to do the dishes!"

Adult: "Oh, yes, you ARE!"

Teen: "Think you're big enough to MAKE ME?"

This teenager is challenging the adult's authority directly, and the way the dialogue ends is the worst possible outcome short of hitting. *Most teenagers—most children, whatever their age—have absolutely no idea how to lose gracefully.* If you back kids into a corner where somebody *must* lose, as the adult does in this dialogue, they feel obligated to keep fighting until either they're overpowered or *you* are. Encounters of that kind, no matter who wins, are never forgotten; they affect the relationship between the adult and the child permanently. For adults to get into such showdowns with children over anything as trivial as whether a chore has been done is a mistake.

The adult in Dialogue 18 sets himself or herself up for trouble by opening the interaction with Blaming, using extra stresses on words and parts of words, and focusing on the personal "you" — turned into "You rotten kid!" by intonation. And everything goes downhill from there. Each Blaming utterance feeds the loop and escalates the hostility, leading straight to the teenager's open declaration of war. I suggest this version:

DIALOGUE 18 REVISITED

Adult: "I see the dishes haven't been done yet." (Leveling)

Teen: "No, they haven't." (Leveling)

Adult: "They need doing." (Computing)

Teen: "I know. But I don't want to do them." (Leveling)

Adult: "Nobody likes to do dishes. That's why communes fail — over who's going to do the dishes." (Computing)

Teen: "Sheeesh . . . I hate dishes!" (Leveling)

Adult: "I hear you." (Leveling)

Teen: "Okay . . . I guess I'll do them." (Leveling)

Adult: "I appreciate that. Thanks." (Leveling)

"I see the dishes haven't been done yet" states only the facts, with neutral intonation, and it makes no accusation. *Saying, "the dishes haven't been done" puts the spotlight on the dishes; "you haven't done the dishes" puts it on the child.* (This is a handy feature of English that adults talking to touchy youngsters should take advantage of. Not all languages allow this kind of foregrounding shift.)

What happens next is important — let's compare the two versions.

ORIGINAL

A: "You haven't done the dishes!"

T: "That's right, I haven't!"

REVISED VERSION

A: "I see the dishes haven't been done yet."

T: "No, they haven't."

In both versions the teen begins by *agreeing*. But notice what the agreement is like in each.

- In the revised version of the dialogue the teen agrees with the adult's statement of the facts. Both adult and teen agree that the dishes are still dirty.

- In the original, on the other hand, the teen agrees with the adult's *anger*. Both adult and teen agree that the two of them are going to *fight*.

✦ The facts are the same in both versions. What triggers the teenager's original metamessage — "So you're going to be angry? O<u>kay</u> — I'll be angry <u>too</u>!" — is the Blaming frame *around* the facts.

No strategic purpose is served by talking angrily before the child has a chance to answer. He might say, "I know that, and I'm sorry — the water's been off all day long." Or, "I'm sorry — I didn't know it was this late. I'll do them right now." Opening in Blamer Mode says, "I'm the adult here, I know in advance that you have <u>no</u> <u>good</u> <u>reason</u> for not doing those dishes, and you're in big <u>trouble</u> with <u>me</u>, buddy!" This *guarantees* a fight, unless the child is incredibly easy to get along with, or wise beyond his years. If the adult asks the question without hostile language and *still* gets a smart-aleck answer, there'll be plenty of time to deal with that.

Notice also that the child in the revised version keeps on trying to get a reaction from the adult. But it doesn't *work*. That's important. *Bad habits that have no payoff will be given up.*

DIALOGUE 19 (with a two-year-old)

Adult: "Time for bed, honey! Let's put your toys away."

Child: "NO!"

Adult: "Not no — yes. You have to go to bed."

Child: "NO! NO! NOOOO!"

Adult: "STOP that!"

Child: "NO! WON'T! WON'T! NO!"

Adult: (*Grim silence, while toddler is hauled away by force.*)

Child: (*Screaming, wailing, shrieking, howling, and kicking.*)

The adult in Dialogue 19 isn't communicating under stress; the opening is pleasant and cheerful and relaxed. When the toddler answers "NO!" (which is two-year-old Blaming) the adult stays neutral but firm. So far, so good. The interaction goes wrong when the adult lets the toddler's escalating Blaming — to two shouted "no"'s and one howled one — to shove him or her over the edge into Blaming *back*. Here's an alternate version of the dialogue:

DIALOGUE 19 REVISITED

Adult: "Time for bed, honey! Let's put your toys away."

Child: "NO!"

Adult: "Not no — yes. It's bedtime."

Child: "NO! NO! NOOOO!"

Adult: "Bedtime, dear. You pick up the blocks and I'll pick up your animals."

Child: "Don't WANT to!"

Adult: "I know. You can play again in the morning. Here's the first block; put it in the toybox, please."

Child: "Don't WANT to!" (*But the child does take the block and puts it in the toy box, and heads back to get more blocks.*)

Both child and adult know, no matter what else goes on, that bed is coming up next. The adult shouldn't be suckered into a fight by somebody not yet three years old, especially over something that isn't even in question. It *scares* kids to find out that they have that much power over adults, who are supposed to be in charge. Children need to be able to feel that the grownups around them know what they're doing, even when the kids would rather they did something else. A child who can get the adult to change the subject from

"Put your toys away and go to bed" to "STOP that [yelling]!" has won a minor — but scary — round. It's better not to let that happen.

DIALOGUE 20 (with a teenage boy)

Adult: "All right, let's get this straightened out! Did you take that dollar bill or not?"

Teen: (*Silence; a fierce glower; arms crossed on chest.*)

Adult: "Please . . . Answer me!"

Teen: (*Silence.*)

Adult: "You're only making this rougher on yourself, don't you know that? And I don't get it! I'm not trying to get you to rat on anybody else, I just want to know if it was you! Why are you being so hard to deal with?"

Teen: (*Silence.*)

Adult: "This kind of thing tears me to pieces! And you KNOW it does! I know I'm handling it all wrong — I always do . . . but I'm doing the best I can! PLEASE don't just sit there like a stone . . ."

The adult in this dialogue is Placating. We don't know what Satir Mode the teenager would use if he were talking, but silences (unless due to physical causes) also have Satir Modes. The most likely choice here is a Blamer silence intended to convey a message of stubborn anger and hostility. The more the adult Placates at him, the angrier the teen is going to get; it's a *totally useless strategy.* No matter how badly the adult needs to know whether the boy is guilty, this won't work. Here's an alternative:

DIALOGUE 20 REVISITED

Adult: "Let's try to get this straightened out. Did you take that money, or not?"

Child: (*Silence; a fierce glower; arms crossed on chest.*)

Adult: "I do have to know; I'd appreciate an answer. Take as much time as you need; I'll wait."

Child: (*Silence.*)

Adult: "(*Silence; waiting.*) All right, if you feel like you can't talk about it now, I won't keep pushing you. Let's drop it for now and plan on bringing it up again right after dinner."

Now the adult is Leveling, which cuts down on the hostility; that's an improvement. Using "let's" instead of direct commands or pleading is also a good move. And the tactic of postponing the blocked discussion — but making *a specific appointment* for reopening it — gives the teenager time to think about what he will say and do.

Now let's go back to Scenario Four and consider how it might have been different if the adults involved had been skilled with the Satir Modes and had used their skill even in that very stressful situation.

Another Look at Scenario Four

At the beginning of Scenario Four, we realize that the confrontation has been going on for some time when we read that Sean's infuriating "So <u>what</u>?" is the "eighth or ninth smart crack in a row." It's significant that it took *that* long for Officer Markson to get rattled. Law enforcement professionals — at a high cost to their health — are trained to keep their language neutral even during intense verbal abuse from private citizens. Markson is well aware that he should keep on resisting the provocation from the two Philips boys; we see him reminding himself repeatedly that it's coming from *children.* When he realizes that he can't control his language any longer, he stops talking to the boys and calls in the parents. By contrast, Mr. and Mrs. Philips — who are under stress that isn't just part of a day's work for them as it is for Officer Markson — lose control of themselves almost immediately. Their efforts to talk to their sons aren't just useless; they actually make matters worse.

In the real world it might take a while to change Sean and Kevin's language behavior. These two boys, unlike the adults, *are* following a deliberate communication strategy. It's one they've had a lot of practice with, and they not only don't *mind* adult opposition to it, that opposition is part of their goal. Getting them to give it up might not work on the first, or even the second or third try. Because we don't have space here to follow several interactions over time, the suggested revisions below will show unrealistically swift changes. Just look at them as the *goals* everyone is working toward. The speedy change shown *is* possible in situations that aren't quite this grim.

The principles this strategy is based on are solid and reliable. Here are the four most important ones:

1. *Anything you feed will grow.* If you want conversation or discussion instead of confrontation, you have to keep that in mind and refuse to be drawn into hostility loops.

2. *The more in the wrong they are, the more most youngsters will fight not to lose face — even if that means getting deeper into trouble.* When adults are trying to get through to children who feel that their backs are to the wall, they have to deliberately structure their language so that the kids won't lose face.

3. *Adults are in charge and are supposed to know what they're doing.* It's their responsibility to provide good communication models for the young people they're talking with and to help the kids when their inexperience is causing dangerous communication problems.

4. *Nothing is more destructive in a discussion between adults and children than framing the interaction as a contest that has to end with a winner and a loser.* Winning and losing are irrelevant when one side — the children — is so completely outranked in the real world.

With these principles in mind, let's consider how the scenario might have gone differently if the adults had made different Satir Mode choices. Here are some possible revisions, with comments.

Revision 1.

Officer: "We had to take the Nelson boy to the emergency room after you two worked him over. Do you understand that?"

The words are the same as in the original scenario, but without all the extra stresses that marked the original as hostile. The officer is Leveling.

Sean: "Yeah. We understand. So what?"

Officer: "When people say 'So what?' it usually means they feel like they have to say something, but they can't think of anything they're happy with."

Instead of using hostile language in response to Sean's sarcasm and Blaming, Markson answers with Computing. He doesn't talk about "you" and "you two"; he doesn't use extra stresses. He talks, neutrally, about hypothetical "people" and what "they" do in hypothetical situations. His lines in the original scenario — "So WHAT? What do you mean . . . " (and so on) fed hostility back to Sean, supplying fuel for the fight and making it easy for the boy to go on with his pose of "I have no feelings and no conscience." The revised lines don't do that.

Sean: "Yeah. Well . . . I'm not happy, that's for sure!"

Officer: "I can believe it. Any special reason?"

Sean: "Because we got caught, damn it! It's not fair!"

Officer: "Maybe. The Nelson kid got beat up; you got caught. That seems fair to me. He didn't want to go to the emergency room; you didn't want to go to jail. Seems to me you're about even."

Markson's strategy of responding in Computer Mode to Sean's hostile language works — the boy shifts to Leveler Mode and the two then set up a Leveling loop, with the truth going in both directions. (This sequence — Blaming or Placating from Speaker A, Computer response from Speaker B, shift to Leveling by Speaker A — is one of the most common outcomes.)

Revision 2.

When Evelyn Philips hears Sean say that the officer's report is true, she instantly goes into full Blaming, with "But how could you POS-

Sibly DO such a horrible thing? What's the MATTER with you boys — have you LOST your MINDS?" This gives the kids, who are already trapped in a situation where the adults have all the real-world power, no option. They either have to admit that what they did was wrong, which is an impossible loss of face for them, or they have to continue the self-destructive game they're playing. A much better move for Evelyn would have been to just say:

"Why, Sean? Why did you and Kevin do that?"

Not "WHY, Sean? WHY did you DO that?" — which has the same words, but is an accusation and an attack, in strong Blamer Mode.

If Evelyn had heard Kevin when he told Markson, "We just did what we had to do, out there," she might have spotted the clue that the officer's anger caused him to miss. Obviously it's important to find out exactly *why* Kevin claims that he and Sean were forced to do what they did. It might be only the street honor code — "He dissed us, and you can't let anybody do that and still hold up your head." But it might also be valuable new information about the events that led up to the violence. It might be information about mitigating circumstances. *But the essential information gets lost when the communication breaks down into verbal violence.*

Revision 3.

In this proposed revision, Evelyn has just completed her long Blaming sequence and asked the boys, "_____ have you LOST your MINDS?"

Sean: "It's no big deal, Mom. Don't make a federal case out of it, okay?"

Kevin: "Yeah, Mom. Nelson's not gonna die or anything."

Father: "I'm trying to understand what you're saying, boys. I think you're saying that as long as you don't kill somebody, it's okay to hurt them — even to hurt them badly. Is that what you meant? Is that right?"

Sean: "Well . . . if they've got it coming, like Nelson did. Yeah. That's how we feel about it."

Father: "Nelson had it coming? Maybe one of you could explain that to me."

David Philips ignores the boys' attempts to provoke him into a fight and stays in Leveler Mode. But he's careful to leave them an illusion of control. He doesn't say he "knows" anything, he says he "thinks." He doesn't ask "Am I right?"; he asks whether "it"—his hypothesis about what the boys are trying to tell him— is right. He doesn't order the boys to explain, he suggests it. And at all times, he uses neutral intonation, so that his words stay nonhostile and no hostility loops are set up.

If things had gone this way, the adults might have found out what the boys had in mind to justify their behavior. They could have explored the situation and perhaps broken through the boys' masks of defiance. There's a difference between "we did it because we had to" and "we did it for a jacket" and "we did it for the hell of it." You can only talk about what happened if you *know* what happened. As long as both boys stay doggedly determined to live up to the cliché—"They showed no remorse"—it's going to be hard to find out the facts. *They have to be persuaded that it's safe to talk.* David Philips' line in the original scenario—"YOU little creeps!", with body language to match—closed off that option.

Is This Coddling?

I want to close this section with a word about a predictable objection: that the revisions I've suggested only show ways for adults to *coddle* young thugs who don't deserve coddling. Youth violence in the United States is out of control; people are angry and at the limits of their patience. The objection is natural. But stop and think, please, before you agree with it. It's important to establish the *purpose* of talking to children in situations like the one in Scenario Four.

The purpose isn't to punish the kids. If they're guilty as charged, they'll be punished by the criminal justice system — and they face a lifetime of other punishments as a result. The purpose isn't to give the adults a chance to express their anger and shock. They're *grown-ups;* they can get along without that for a little while.

The purpose of talking to children in crises like the one shown in Scenario Four is to achieve three goals:

1. To find out *exactly* what happened.

2. To determine accurately how the children feel about what they did.

3. To persuade the kids that *their* best choice is to cooperate with the adults who are handling the situation.

That's not coddling; that's efficiency and good sense. None of these goals is possible when communication is allowed to degenerate into combat.

Talking to the Cyberchild

The child who's involved in online communication will have learned a *lot* about the difference between "Why did you say that?" (Leveling) and "WHY did you SAY that?!" (Blaming or Placating). When people talk face to face, their body language lets you know which of these utterances you're dealing with, but online you only have the words. Writing all in capital letters online is considered yelling, but no agreed-upon system for making intonation clear in writing exists. This has caused cybertalkers so much trouble that they've invented a set of typed squiggles called *emoticons* to help with it. For example, " : -) " means "I'm smiling as I write this" and " : - (" means "I'm frowning as I write this." (Look at the colon-hyphen-parentheses sequences sideways and you'll see why.) This means that when you hear a cyberchild using what sounds like hostile language, you can say, "Wait a minute. Is that with a smiley-face or one of the others?"

Cyberkids who spend a lot of time playing computer games are likely to become highly skilled at logical reasoning, which means they're more likely to *debate* adults than other children. There's a serious risk that they'll be *better* at this than the adults — who don't have much time for computer games — are. They'll be extremely good at spotting patterns like an adult's shift to Computer Mode, and may trap you in what appears to be an eternal Computing loop. When either of these things happens:

✦ Don't get mad. Or, if you can't *help* getting mad — do what you can to keep that to yourself. The youngster was playing a game with you and will consider himself or herself the *winner* if you lose your cool.

State the facts, and nothing but the facts, like this, in Leveler Mode:

"You're good at debating, and you've won the debate. Congratulations. But adults who lose debates with kids are even less likely to let the kids shave their heads than they would be if that hadn't happened."

That tells the youngster: "You won the debate, but you lost the game. Maybe next time you see a chance to make somebody who outranks you lose face you'll want to handle it differently."

Note. I want to make one thing clear before we go on to Chapter 5: Nobody "is" a Blamer or a Placater or a Leveler. The Satir Modes aren't character or personality traits. Saying "a Blamer" is just shorthand for "a person who at a particular time is using the language pattern called Blaming." Statements like "My son's a Blamer, but my daughter's a Leveler" are tempting and are a common error; they're never accurate. Resist the temptation.

+

I don't feel like you see what I'm saying!

Using the Sensory Modes

--- Scenario Five ---

Grace Wainwright had been Laura Beckett's homeroom teacher for almost six months now; nothing Laura said or did surprised her any more. The *last* thing she wanted to do was lose her temper now. The whole point of this conference was to convince Laura that control belonged to her teachers and parents and not to her fourteen-year-old self. But Grace was finding it hard to stay calm, and she could see that Mrs. Beckett was even more upset than she was.

"Laura," Grace said slowly, "can't you see our point of view at all? Your mother and I only want the best for you . . . can't you see that? We're trying to help. But if you go on refusing even to try to look at things reasonably _____ "

Laura laughed and muttered something under her breath.

"What?" Grace asked. "What was that?"

"I *said*, you wanta help me, get off my back."

"But, Laura _____ "

The teenager tossed back her hair. "You and Mom are just like everybody else," she sneered. "You guys just want to push me around!"

"Laura Elizabeth!" Christine Becket snapped, closing her eyes briefly, as if she were in pain. She *was* in pain; it *hurt* to have her daughter act like this. "Why must you always look at the whole world as a personal conspiracy against you? Don't you see how conceited that is?"

Grace took a deep breath and tried again. "Laura," she said, "The way your mother and I see it is simple. We don't expect miracles. All we're asking you to do is be in your classes when you're supposed to be and do your homework."

Silence. Laura stared fixedly at the floor.

"<u>Look</u> at your teacher when she talks to you!" said her mother sharply." And have the decency to _____ "

"I'm as decent as <u>you</u> two are!" the girl said defiantly.

"Laura," Grace protested, "<u>that</u> kind of remark does <u>not</u> <u>help</u>! You're <u>not</u> a stupid girl, I cannot see why _____ "

"<u>Sure</u> I'm stupid!" Laura said, cutting her off. "You put your finger right on the problem <u>that</u> time, Miss Wainwright. I'm <u>stupid</u>. Can't you people get that through your <u>heads</u>?"

"Laura," her mother said, through her teeth, "that's ridiculous!" Now, are you going to go to your classes and do your work, or <u>not</u>?"

"<u>Not</u>!" Laura announced emphatically. "<u>I'm</u> stupid and all that stuff the teachers give me to <u>do</u> is stupid. I'm not doing <u>any</u> of it. And you can't <u>make</u> me!"

The two women looked at each other in despair.

"You are <u>impossible</u> to talk to, Laura!" said the teacher bitterly, and Christine Beckett nodded her agreement. It was true.

———————————————— ✦ ————————————————

What's Going On Here?

This sorry situation isn't unusual. Here are three people, two adults and a teenager, doing the very best they can to get along in this world and to communicate with each other. *But it just isn't working.* Why?

The Teacher's Point of View

Grace Wainwright doesn't *know* why they keep trying to talk to Laura; it certainly doesn't seem to be doing any good. For any student willing to try, Grace is ready to go more than halfway, as many times as it takes. But trying to help Laura Beckett seems like a total waste of time that could be spent helping youngsters who *want* to be helped.

Grace is just about ready to give up. Only three things are stopping her. (1) Because she knows that she really dislikes Laura, she doesn't trust herself to be fair. (2) Laura's not a delinquent. She's not taking drugs or running with a gang. She's uncooperative and stubborn and hostile and *difficult,* but no more than that. And (3) Laura's mother and father are clearly worried and willing to help.

But Grace doesn't know what any of the adults involved can or should do next. Laura *is* impossible to talk to!

The Parent's Point of View

Christine Beckett loves Laura and has tried hard to raise her properly. But somehow, although Laura's two older brothers turned out well, neither she nor her husband have had much luck dealing with their daughter. They've even tried professional counseling, but that didn't help either. It's as if Laura came from a different planet and still lives in a different world. Christine wouldn't blame Miss Wainwright for giving up on the child. The question is: What are they going to *do*?

The Child's Point of View

When Laura looks at her mother and her teacher, she doesn't see two caring adults bending over backwards to help her. She would say "I know my parents love me — but that's just because I'm their kid. They don't <u>like</u> me. And my teachers don't like me. <u>Nobody</u> likes me!" But she doesn't know <u>why</u>. It seems to Laura that she's been in trouble ever since she was born, without ever understanding what it is she's doing wrong. It's as if everybody else is playing some kind of mysterious game and they're punishing her because she doesn't know how to play — but they won't tell her what the rules are. Laura follows the rules she understands, the ones about drugs and sex and violence, but she doesn't feel that she gets credit for that. Other kids, lots of them doing things that are really bad, get treated better than she does. People say she doesn't try — Laura knows that she *has* tried, over and over again. All anybody ever does is tell her to stop being such a pain in the neck.

Laura *isn't* stupid. The way she perceives it, if people are going to treat her like dirt, she'll just stay out of their way; all she asks is that they let her alone. If Laura had to sum up her life in ten words or less, she would say: "I just don't get it, that's all!"

Sometimes the reasons behind a scenarios like this one are obvious to everybody and easy to understand. For example, communication problems are predictable:

- When the child you can't communicate with is emotionally disturbed

- When the child has a physical or mental disability

- When the child is deeply involved in criminal behavior

- When the parents are in the midst of a messy divorce

But Laura is a healthy normal young girl with no delinquent tendencies, living in a good home with loving parents and going to a pretty good school. Under *these* conditions it's hard to understand why the adults and the child can't find a way to communicate successfully.

In a situation like this one, when nothing seems to work and there seems to be no reason for the failure, adults should try focusing not on the child's personality or character, but on the child's *language*, looking for patterns that might give some clue to the source of the trouble. In this chapter we'll look at one of the most obvious of those patterns, to see how our knowledge about it can be used to break through the walls that children like Laura routinely set up between themselves and adults who would like to help.

What to Do About It—Using the Sensory Modes

Talking Senses

Suppose somebody has told you about a plan and asked you for your opinion; suppose the plan pleases you. There are literally an infinite number of things you could say that would carry that message. Here are some likely possibilities:

"I see exactly what you mean; I can just *picture* it! It looks to me like you've solved the problem!"

"That sounds terrific—it really rings a bell with me! It sounds to me like you've solved the problem!"

"That feels exactly right to me; you put your finger right on the heart of the problem! I feel like you've solved it!"

When you look at these three utterances, you immediately notice that they carry the same message, but they're different in one important way: *Each one uses the vocabulary from a different sensory system of the human body.* The first one uses sight vocabulary, the second hearing, and the third the vocabulary of touch. We call these vocabularies the *sensory modes,* and we can use them systematically to make communication easier.

Human beings face a constant flood of information, made up of hundreds of thousands of separate perceptions and sensations daily. If we tried to deal with all or even most of them, we'd collapse. We have to filter them down to a manageable number, choosing those we can forget, those we need to respond to, and those to index and store in memory. To do this amazing task, we use our brain and our sensory systems: sight, hearing, touch, taste, smell, and roughly a dozen other less familiar ones.

By the time we are about five or six, we've discovered that one of our sensory systems (almost always sight, hearing, or touch) is more useful to us than the others. When we use that system we understand more quickly and easily, and we respond and remember better. When we can, that's the sensory system we rely on; when that's not possible, we're less at ease and we have to try harder.

This sensory preference or dominance is reflected in our language behavior, particularly when we're tense or under stress. And unlike the Satir Modes, our preference for a particular sensory mode is independent of the situations we find ourself in. A sight dominant person who has to carry out a task in the dark will rely on the senses of hearing and touch because there's no choice—but that person will still be sight dominant. Sensory dominance is an across-the-board phenomenon, not a shifting one like Satir Mode preferences.

Kindergarten teachers and primary caregivers can sort small children out for you on this basis. They say things like these:

> "There's no point at all in trying to tell Jerry how to do that. Unless he has something to <u>look</u> at, he's not going to understand what you're telling him." (That is: Jerry is a *sight dominant* child.)

> "You're wasting your time showing Nancy those pictures — you'll have to <u>tell</u> her exactly what you want, or she's not going to understand." (That is: Nancy is *hearing dominant.*)

> "It does no good to explain a task to Marilyn, and you can show her pictures till you're blue in the face — it won't work. She never really understands unless she can get right in there with both hands and <u>do</u> it, hands on." (That is: Marilyn is a *touch dominant* youngster.)*

The reason the sensory modes are so important in communication is that they're like very small languages. When you know that a child speaks only Japanese, you don't try to talk to him in French; when you know that a child whose native language is Spanish speaks only a little English, you try to speak to her in Spanish, especially when you know she's anxious. The sensory modes are of course not French and Spanish and Japanese, but the *metaphor* is accurate. Talking to children in their preferred sensory modes helps them understand and respond to what you say. Talking to them in a *different* sensory mode, especially when communication is difficult anyway, is like talking to them in a foreign language. The scale of the problem is very different, but the principle is the same.

---

*You may come across other terms for sensory preferences, such as "visual" for sight, "auditory" for hearing, and "kinesthetic," "tactile," and "tactual" for touch. There's general agreement on what the eye and ear terms mean. However, some who use "kinesthetic," "tactile," or "tactual" include "feelings" in the sense of *emotions* under those headings. They would say that words like "guilt" and "happiness" and "fear" come from the touch vocabulary. The *Gentle Art of Verbal Self-Defense* system doesn't do this; in a sequence such as "I feel happy," only the word "feel" would be considered a touch mode item.

If you go back and look at the vocabulary used by each of the speakers in Scenario Five, you'll notice that both adults in this very tense situation rely heavily on *eye* vocabulary. Laura, on the other hand, uses mostly touch vocabulary. This mismatch makes the stress worse for all three, making communication even more difficult — which increases the stress again, and so on round the loop. This is called *sensory mode mismatch.* It's a very common problem in communication under stress. It should be avoided whenever that's possible — and it almost always *is* possible. Consider these interactions, for example.

SENSORY MODE MATCHING

Child: "How does it look?" (Sight)

Adult: "It looks great to me. Good work!" (Sight)

SENSORY MODE MISMATCH

Child: "How does it look?" (Sight)

Adult: "I feel like you're doing really well. Good work!" (Touch)

SENSORY-NEUTRAL COMMUNICATION

Child: "How does it look?" (Sight)

Adult: "I think it's fine. Good work!" (No sensory words.)

Responding to the Sensory Modes

You'll automatically recognize an English sensory mode you're hearing or reading because you speak English fluently; you don't have to go look it up anywhere. And the information in the examples just given is enough to let us work out the rules for responding. They are:

✦ RULE ONE: Match the sensory mode coming at you.

✦ RULE TWO: If you can't follow rule one, try to avoid sensory mode mismatch by using as little sensory vocabulary as possible.

People who are relaxed and at ease shift from one sensory mode to another without difficulty, using all of the sensory vocabularies at will, just as I'm doing here. It's only in communication under stress that the strong preference for one sensory mode becomes important. However, because communication between adults and children so often *is* stressful, the sensory mode technique is valuable for everybody.

The Special Problem of Touch Dominance

Children who prefer sight mode or hearing mode are on roughly equal footing in our society, though sight outranks hearing in our culture in many ways. But touch dominant children are in a different situation, and they face serious problems. We are a "Don't touch!" culture. We would never send children to school wearing blindfolds or earplugs, ordering them to keep their eyes and ears to themselves while they learn. We expect them to look and listen with their full attention, believing that's necessary if they're to master the material being taught. But we *do* send touch dominant children to school as if they were wearing heavy mittens, ordered to keep their hands to themselves, demanding all the while that they compete with the sight and hearing dominant children.

This is truly unfair. The sight dominant child's eagerness to look is rewarded; the hearing dominant child's eagerness to listen is praised. But the touch dominant child's eagerness to *touch* almost always gets a negative reaction. The swift rebukes — "Johnny! No touching!" and "Mary! Keep your fingers off that!" — do nothing to make children relaxed and comfortable so that they will be able to use *all* their sensory vocabularies. Instead, they lead to anxious children who — like Laura in Scenario Five — feel that they're always in trouble, usually without understanding what it is exactly that they're doing wrong. By the time they're teenagers they've been rejected so often and so emphatically that they're convinced they can't do anything right.

Years of negative experiences won't melt away from a child's memory just because an adult matches sensory modes. This technique is not magic, and much patient effort will be needed to turn the child around. But sensory mode matching is a powerful tool. It will help you get past the barriers such children raise in communication. It will help you earn their trust, so that they will both talk to you and listen when you talk to them. This helps. You still have all the tasks of persuading the child, negotiating with the child, and so forth, but now there's a far better chance for *real* communication between you. This is especially important for adults who spend a lot of time with touch dominant youngsters, because those kids must deal with so much rejection elsewhere.

Now let's look at a set of dialogues in which the way the sensory modes are used makes a significant difference.

Sample Dialogues

DIALOGUE 21 (with an eight-year-old)

Child: "I don't get this. It's too <u>hard</u>."

Adult: "The only reason you're having trouble with that is because you aren't <u>looking</u> at it! It's not written on the <u>floor</u>, you know — it's right there in front of your eyes, on the <u>page</u>!"

Child: "No . . . I just don't <u>get</u> it!"

Adult: "Look, quit saying 'I don't get it' and keep your eyes on your <u>work</u>! <u>Hon</u>estly!"

This is the most typical of all sensory-mode-mismatch dialogues. All over the English-speaking world, every single day, eye or ear dominant adults are trying to convince touch dominant children that they *would* "get it" if they would only *look* at it (or *listen* to it.)

To the adults the children's repeated "I don't get it!"'s seem so unreasonable that it's infuriating — after all, how *could* they understand without looking or listening? The tension this causes locks both the adults and the children into their preferred (and clashing) sensory modes, which increases the tension and locks them in more tightly still, which . . . And so on round the loop. The adults then perceive the children as lazy and stubborn and totally unwilling to try, while the children perceive the adults as mean. This is a problem of language that is almost always mistaken for a problem of *character.* In all such situations, instead of feeding the loop, the adults should switch to touch mode to find out if sensory mode mismatch is at least partly responsible for the breakdown, as in the following dialogue:

DIALOGUE 21 REVISITED

Child: "I don't get this. It's too <u>hard</u>."

Adult: "Maybe I can put my finger on what's giving you such a rough time — I'll be glad to try. What is it exactly that you don't get?"

Child: "It's this stuff . . . right here." (*Points.*)

Adult: "Hmmmm . . . let's go over it together; I'm sure you can do it."

And what if the child *isn't* touch dominant? What if the problem really is laziness or a learning disorder or something else entirely? If you just switch to touch mode, don't you risk missing some serious problem? *No.* If touch dominance isn't what's causing the trouble, you'll have done no harm, but it won't help either. And that will tell you to look for some other cause.

DIALOGUE 22 (with a thirteen-year-old)

Mother: "Now, let me see . . . The first thing we have to do is decide on the <u>col</u>ors you want for your room. What do you think? What would look best?"

Child: "I don't care."

Mother: "Of <u>course</u> you care! It's important to have colors that <u>you</u> can be happy with! Now help me out, Janice — how about a sort of Wedgwood blue for the walls, and maybe a slightly darker shade for the rug?"

Child: "Okay."

Mother: "Okay? That's <u>all</u> . . . o<u>kay</u>? Look, if I'm willing to spend the time and money to see that you have a pretty room, the <u>least</u> you could do is <u>cooperate</u> just a little bit! How can you be so un<u>grate</u>ful?"

Child: "But I don't know what you want me to <u>say</u>!"

Mother: "It's not what <u>I</u> want, it's what <u>you</u> want! And I can't even beGIN doing your room over unless I know what COL-·ORS you want!"

Child: "Honestly . . . You pick them. No kidding, it doesn't make any difference to me!"

Mother: "OH! That is just riDICulous! WHY do you keep saying things like that??!"

Our preferred sensory systems do seem to us to be the only *possible* choice. We can't believe that the information that matters so much to us — as colors do for this exasperated adult — matters hardly at all to somebody else. Nevertheless, that's how it is. The ear dominant child above truly does not care how her room is going to *look.* When she says she doesn't care what paints and fabrics the adult picks, she's just telling the truth. And she's baffled when that sets her mother off the way it does. *What,* she wonders, *does having no color preferences have to do with being grateful?*

The child is right. Apply Miller's Law (p. 28) here. Assume that what she says is true; what could it be true *of?* Obviously, it would be true of a world where sight isn't the most important tool for processing information — the world of a child who isn't sight dominant. The adult should say this to the child:

"I'm going to use one shade of blue for the walls, and a darker one for everything else. This is your chance to tell me if you don't want me to do that . . . No? No objections? Okay, that's decided, then. Now let's talk about what kind of stereo you want and where you're going to put it."

If the adult wants the child to enjoy (and take care of) the redecorated room, this is the only way to go. Money for things-to-see isn't nearly as important as money for things-to-hear. Janice's mother will need to remember that this will hold true for such matters as choosing clothing, picking out greeting cards, and planning a party or a wedding. Things that are critically important to the adult will be things the child has no interest in. Not because Janice is ungrateful and uncooperative, but because visual information — information for the eye — just doesn't matter to her.

Note: The child in the dialogue is a young girl, but could just as easily be a boy. There's no evidence that any sensory preference is more likely for one gender than for the other.

DIALOGUE 23

Adult: "Look, Tracy, I know I said you should make yourself comfortable here, but you can't possibly address those envelopes right with that radio going all the time."

Teen: "Yes, I can, Mr. Smith. Really I can!"

Adult: "Sorry. I don't want to seem rigid, but you'll have to turn off that noise so that you can give your full attention to what you're doing."

Teen: (*Sighs.*) "Yes, sir."

Mr. Smith is mistaken: this ear dominant youngster will do *better* work with some ear input.

Hard as it is for people who aren't hearing dominant to believe, the "noise" actually helps; it's easier for most ear dominant people to do visual work with a radio playing. In the same way, it's helpful to most touch dominant people to be able to knit or doodle or take notes while they listen to a lecture or watch a film. The sensory input that would be distracting to a person who prefers the sense of sight isn't interference for people whose preferences are different.

There's no need to revise this dialogue. This interaction shouldn't happen at all, unless the employer really does notice that the youngster is neglecting the work that's supposed to be done.

Let's go back now to Scenario Five and consider how it might have gone differently if the sensory mode technique had been added to the language mix.

Another Look at Scenario Five

Grace Wainwright opens the conversation in sight mode. The visual words and phrases are in italics below.

"Laura, can't you *see* our *point of view* at all? Your mother and I only want the best for you . . . can't you *see* that? We're trying to <u>help</u>. But if you go on refusing even to <u>try</u> to *look* at things rationally _____"

Laura's mother does the same thing:

"<u>Why</u> must you always *look* at the whole world as a personal conspiracy against you? Don't you *see* how <u>conceited</u> <u>that</u> <u>is</u>?"

Laura's own speech, however—when she's willing to talk at all—is in touch mode. Here's the entire list of Laura's utterances, with the touch items in italics.

"I <u>said</u>, you wanta help me, *get off my back.*"

"You and Mom are just like everybody else . . . you just want to *push me around.*"

"I'm as decent as <u>you</u> two are!" (Sensory neutral.)

"<u>Sure</u> I'm stupid. You *put your finger right on the problem* <u>that</u> time, Miss Wainwright. I'm <u>stupid</u>. Can't you people *get that through your heads?*"

"<u>Not</u>! <u>I'm</u> stupid, all that stuff the teachers give me to <u>do</u> is stupid. I'm not doing <u>any</u> of it. And you can't make me." (Sensory neutral, unless we count all those "do"'s as touch-related.)

The sensory mode clash between Laura and the two adults isn't French going one way and Chinese coming back. But it's a striking example of a pattern that reliably interferes with communication, being used at a time when that's the last thing these three people need.

Suppose they had known and used the sensory mode rules. Suppose Laura had made the effort to match the adults' sight mode, or they had switched to her preferred touch mode. How might the scenario have been different?

Here are some likely revisions.

IF LAURA SWITCHES TO SIGHT MODE TO MATCH THE ADULTS

Teacher: "Laura, can't you see our point of view at all? Your mother and I want only the best for you . . . can't you see that? We're trying to <u>help</u>. But if you go on refusing even to <u>try</u> to look at things rationally _____ "

Laura: "The way <u>I</u> see it, you're <u>not</u> trying to help me! I wish you'd both just leave me alone."

Teacher: "But Laura, if we do that — if we just ignore you — won't it look to you as if we don't care?"

Laura: "Maybe. I guess so. But I see things really <u>differently</u> from the way you and Mom see them!"

Teacher: "We know that, Laura — that's why we have to talk. That's why we need your help. If we all had the same picture of the situation, we wouldn't <u>need</u> a conference. Can you agree with that?"

Laura: "Okay. I see what you mean."

IF THE ADULTS SWITCH TO TOUCH MODE TO MATCH LAURA

Laura: "I <u>said</u>, you wanta help me, get off my back."

Teacher: "Is that how you feel, Laura? Like your mother and I are just weighing you down?"

Laura: "Yeah . . . that, and pushing me around."

Teacher: "That's rough. But I think you're wrong. And I feel sure I can get you to understand <u>why</u> you're wrong, if you'll let me."

Laura: "I know how everybody feels about me! What's the point of running me into the ground all the time? It's not like I didn't <u>know</u>!"

Mother: "Hold on a minute, Laura. We're not here to run you into the ground. We're here to try to get a handle on what's making things so hard for you, so we can help. Try to give us a little room, okay?"

Laura: "Okay. I'm sorry. It's just . . . I just seem to rub everybody the wrong way all the time. I get so mad, I don't feel like going to class or anything else. I just feel like putting it all out of my mind so I don't have to think about it."

Teacher: "Can you put your finger on the problem for us, Laura? I mean, what's the <u>heaviest</u> problem for you?"

Laura: "The problem is: I just don't <u>get</u> it!"

These revisions don't work a miracle. Laura and the adults will still have to work their way through Laura's resistance. But as long as they're talking, progress is possible. You'll also notice that the talk doesn't stay *hostile*. Everybody is distressed by the situation, but they're not *angry*.

I know from long experience that your immediate reaction as you read the second revision may have been that the adults switched not to touch language but to *crude* language. If that describes your feelings accurately, please stop and think about it for a minute. *Because that typical reaction is part of the burden of rejection that touch dominant children have to deal with every day of their lives.* The touch vocabulary in everyday use (as opposed to the specialized vocabularies of sculpture or surgery or geology) is often perceived very negatively by eye and ear dominant people.

There's no rational reason for that reaction; it's something learned in school, and is in most ways as much a matter of fashion as hemlines are. It's important when communicating with touch dominant youngsters to try hard to put "I get it" on an equal level with "I see" and "I understand." You're not trying to make a speech; you're trying to help a child who's having a hard time communicating.

Because Laura is the child here, it's not reasonable to expect *her* to make the sensory mode switch. The adults should take the responsibility for the change, however awkward they may feel using the sensory mode they like the least.

People hearing about sensory mode matching for the first time often say, "It's too easy! Nothing that easy could possibly work!" So many things are so difficult — be glad that a technique as easy as this one *does* work.

When you're interacting with a child who's using touch mode — or who's relying entirely on the language of the body and refusing to use any words at all — you can always try the sensory mode technique. If mode mismatch isn't part of the problem, it won't help, but it won't do any harm. And when it does work, it works wonders.

Talking to the Cyberchild

Most cyberkids are going to be either sight dominant or touch dominant. For the visual kids, the computer makes even their "talking" into visual information and offers them a whole array of resources for making pictures and other graphics. For the touch dominant ones, the constant handling of the mouse and/or keyboard is a pleasure (though they'll fuss about "bad" keyboards that don't provide much tactile feedback). And the social awkwardness touch dominant children develop from encountering so much rejection is less of a handicap online than face to face. The sight dominant child will want a computer that offers good color and pictures. To the touch dominant child the most important thing will be the way the keyboard and the mouse feel.

To convince hearing dominant children that computers are important — so they won't end up excluded from the information revolution — buy them a computer with a good sound system, one that will play music. If you can manage the cost, get one that will let *them* play music. And use those features as your selling points, like this:

> "Listen, I know you don't care anything about most computer stuff — that's okay. But do something for me — just *listen* to this one. You can play your stereo through it. And you can use it like a synthesizer. Listen to this . . ."

—————————— ✦ ——————————

CHAPTER 6

I don't want to hear you SAY that!

Special Communication Problems

We've been exploring the serious problem of adult–child communication breakdown and its consequences. You're now equipped with accurate information about language learning and language behavior. And you've learned these five specific techniques for improving communication between adults and children:

1. Using the language traffic rules

2. Managing the English Verbal Attack Patterns

3. Using three-part messages

4. Using the Satir Modes

5. Using the sensory modes

With this foundation to work from, we can now move on to consider some special problems that adults who interact with youngsters must face today.

Sample Dialogues

DIALOGUE 24: "Why Should I Be Sorry? I Don't Care!" (with a **twelve-year-old girl who's been caught shoplifting in a small-town grocery store, and has never done anything like this before)**

Mother: "I am just <u>sick</u> about this, Charlotte . . . It's not just <u>you</u>, you know. It's <u>all</u> of us. Your whole family! How are your sisters, and your father and I, supposed to hold up our HEADS in this town when everybody <u>knows</u> <u>what</u> <u>you've</u> DONE?"

Child: "So I <u>took</u> a couple of <u>can</u>dy bars! Big <u>deal</u>! It wasn't exactly a major <u>bank</u> robbery, you know!"

Mother: "Charlotte, shoplifting is STEALing! It's a CRIME! It's terribly, terribly WRONG! You've disgraced your whole family, and we ALL will have to pay for what you've done! But that seems to be oKAY with you! You're not one BIT sorry, ARE you?"

Child: (*Shrugs elaborately, and stares at the wall.*) "Why should I be <u>sorry</u>? <u>I</u> don't care!"

As in Scenario Four, where two young boys had beaten another boy badly and claimed not to care, it's *possible* that Charlotte's speaking the truth. Young people do exist who can't feel empathy and guilt, who lack all moral sense, and who need medical attention for this deformity of the spirit. People who have to communicate with such youngsters have a very hard row to hoe. If you *do* face that task, the techniques in this book will be helpful to you — but you also need expert help from professionals trained for such situations. For the dialogues in this chapter, we'll assume that we're discussing normal healthy children. With that in mind, let's see just what the mother in the dialogue is dealing with.

We know children aren't born indifferent to others' feelings. Children may be born with the potential for sin, but they aren't born knowing how. Children aren't born cruel and callous; they have to be taught to be that way. Many research studies have proved that children who are barely able to crawl will try to comfort another child who's crying. If that doesn't work, and if no adult offers help, they'll start crying, too, in sympathy. *The only exception to this is children who come from abusive homes, who not only won't try to help but may even push or hit the other child.* We can safely assume that Charlotte does care about the pain she's causing her family. The question then is: Why did she do what she did and why won't she say she's sorry?

The obvious and tempting answer — that she's just a rotten kid, just plain *bad* — should be the answer you accept when there aren't any other possibilities. I can think of at least four other explanations — not excuses, *explanations* — for Charlotte's behavior.

1. Charlotte stole the candy bars as part of an "entrance requirement" to join a gang, or under some other kind of peer pressure. In this case, she'll feel that she *had* to steal the candy, in spite of the risks.

2. She's a child for whom the problems of her daily life have become so overwhelming and so terrifying that she desperately wants adult intervention. The shoplifting is her way of letting the adults around her know that she needs and wants help.

3. She's a child who feels rejected by those she loves, perhaps because she thinks her parents love her sisters but don't love her. The shoplifting is her way of expressing her pain, or punishing her family for the rejection, or both.

4. She's a child who feels that nobody notices her, that she is a kind of invisible person always on the edge of whatever is happening. The shoplifting is an attempt to get attention — *any* kind of attention. If it has to be negative, she still thinks that's better than none at all.

Any of these explanations could be correct. And except for the first one (peer pressure), Charlotte may have very little conscious awareness of her own reasons. An adult who wants to find out what's going on with her will have to do two things: get past the barrier that's making it hard for her to communicate at *all,* and help her understand her own feelings well enough so that she knows what she wants to say. *Neither* of those things can happen in an atmosphere like that in Dialogue 24.

Charlotte's mother opens her conversation with her daughter like this:

Mother: "I am just <u>sick</u> about this, Charlotte . . . It's not just <u>you</u>, you know. It's <u>all</u> of us. Your whole family! How are your sisters, and your father and I, supposed to hold up our HEADS in this town when everybody <u>knows</u> what you've DONE?"

This is Blaming. It's intended to make Charlotte feel guilty and ashamed, not only for having stolen the candy, but for the disgrace she's brought on her family. If it were Leveling instead of Blaming, it would be less likely to force Charlotte into defensive posturing. Here's a Leveling version of the message:

Mother: "I'm sick about this, Charlotte. It's not just you, it's all of us. Our whole family is going to have trouble holding up our heads in this town when everybody knows what you've done."

Now we've gotten rid of all those extra emphatic stresses, and that's a lot better. But there's another serious problem with the original utterance: *It ends with a question that Charlotte can't possibly answer.* Maybe the mother was really looking for an answer; maybe she was asking what's called a *rhetorical* question and didn't expect an answer. Either way, she leaves Charlotte with nothing to say back. Adults who ask children such questions should remember that they *always* create communication gridlock. They're like pulling your car crossways in front of your child's car at an intersection and ordering the child to drive right on through.

With the "How can we possibly hold up our HEADS?" question out of the way, Charlotte could answer with, "I know that, Mother, and I'm sorry." She may not be willing to, but the change makes it *possible.*

Now please look at the mother's second utterance:

Mother: "Charlotte, shoplifting is STEALing! It's a CRIME! It's terribly, terribly WRONG! You've disgraced your whole family, and we ALL will have to pay for what YOU have done! But that seems to be oKAY with you! You're not one BIT sorry, ARE you?"

Once again we have nothing but Blaming, and it's more intense than it was at the beginning — which is what always happens when Blaming is met with Blaming. A hostility loop has been set up and the Blaming has escalated.

To make things even worse, the mother has asked another unwise question — the *negative* question, "You're not one BIT sorry, ARE you?" Its metamessage is, "Don't you dare try to tell me you're sorry, because I know in advance that you're NOT." Which again leaves Charlotte with nothing to say, because both "Yes, I am sorry" and "No, I'm not sorry" are *wrong*. Whatever the reasons for Charlotte's behavior, everything her mother says makes it harder and harder for the child to *state* them, even if she's consciously aware of them.

Charlotte's mother wants to hear a response something like this:

"Mother, I know that what I did has caused you great pain and will continue to be a problem for everyone in our family. I am sorrier than I can even begin to tell you. What I'd like to do now, if you'll let me, is explain <u>why</u> I did something so dreadful."

There are two things the mother either has forgotten or doesn't know. First, it's unreasonable for an adult whose own utterances are so badly flawed to expect a twelve-year-old child—for whom she has been the language *model*—to come up with a speech like that. Where is Charlotte supposed to have learned *how*? It's unfair and irrational for the mother to expect the child to communicate more expertly than she herself does. Second, the more upset Charlotte is, the less likely she is to have the kind of detachment and calmness it takes to put together an answer like the one shown, and all that Blaming isn't going to calm the child down. Here's the basic principle to remember:

✦ To communicate with a child in trouble, who will already be frightened and confused, you have to establish that it's *safe* to talk to you.

You can't do that by shaming and lecturing, no matter how much the child deserves it. If your goal is to punish and/or scare the child, that's different. But if your goal is to establish good solid communication, all those negative messages only stand in your way. And you must always ask yourself: *"If I say this thing, what options does the child have? What are the possible replies? What can the child say <u>back</u>?"* When everything you say pushes the child into a corner, increases the distress, and cuts off the range of possible responses, you make communication impossible. You can't expect children to rise above the situation and take care of the communication problems; that's a job for grownups.

Consider this revision of Dialogue 24.

Mother: "I am just <u>sick</u> about this, Charlotte. I won't pretend I'm not. It's going to be hard for all of us to face other people in this town now; I'm sure you know that. And it's going to be hardest of all for <u>you</u>."

Child: "So I took a couple of candy bars. Big <u>deal</u>! It wasn't exactly a major <u>bank</u> robbery, you know."

Mother: "Charlotte, when people feel bad about something they've done, especially if they're scared, they say things they don't really mean. I know you're sorry, and I know you know that shoplifting isn't trivial. Do you want to talk to me about it?"

Child: (*Shrugs elaborately, and stares at the wall.*) "I don't know what to <u>say</u>!"

Mother: "What I'd really like to know — if <u>you</u> know — is <u>why</u> you took the candy. Take your time, honey; I'll wait. We have all the time in the world."

DIALOGUE 25: "I Wish I Was Dead"

To hear a child say, "I wish I was dead," is either infuriating or frightening; what matters is *which one*. Children who say this without meaning it need to learn that it's unacceptable and may cause big problems later at a time when they really want to convince adults they need help. Children who say it and *do* mean it are giving the adults around them an opportunity that *must not* be missed: a chance to find out what's causing them to feel suicidal and take steps to correct that.

One of the most tragic cross-generation communication breakdowns is the "If we'd only known!" disaster that seems to adults to come out of nowhere. Like the suicide after which parents and teachers say, "But the child never said a <u>word</u>! Sure, there were normal problems, like you have with any kid, but we had no idea anything <u>serious</u> was going on! If we'd only <u>known</u>!"

How can such a terrible thing happen? Look at the following dialogue, between a parent and a nine-year-old boy.

Child: "I wish I was dead."

Adult: "Uhuh."

Child: "I said, I _____"

Adult: "Hey, you can see how busy I am! Find something to do, Tommy, please. Don't be a pest."

Child: "Okay. Sorry."

Adult: "Thank you, Tommy; I appreciate it."

This adult isn't being verbally abusive; the language isn't Blaming, it's Leveling. When a child has interrupted over and over and has been listened to each time, the adult's response may be justified. But it should not happen the *first* time the child interrupts, or the second time, especially if the child has come looking for the adult. And no matter what the circumstances: Before cutting off communication, the adult must be sure to *listen*! I once heard a woman answer her child's "I wish I was dead" with "I wish I were dead, dear"; that's parental malpractice.

Good communication habits have to be established early. Children need to grow up knowing that, within reasonable limits, the adults around them will listen when they talk and that there won't be *penalties* for talking. If their attempts to talk are always ignored, or are met with brush-offs or ridicule or interrogations, they'll stop trying.

That's very convenient when children are small and their chatter is a nuisance. I understand that well, because when I went back to college to finish my degree, I had five small kids at home. I wrote my thesis (and my first book) with a whole houseful of them racing back and forth. But having kids who've given up trying to talk to you is dangerous. And saying "Why didn't you tell us?" when the child's attempts to communicate have never been welcome before is ridiculous. It's also important to remember the results of current research: Studies show that the *first three years* of a child's life are the most important ones. Adults who decide not to talk to kids until they're older and more interesting need to keep that in mind.

✦ The only appropriate response to anything even remotely like "I wish I was dead" — from your child or any other child — is "Tell me about that, please," and your full attention.

If the response you get is "I can't write my book report!" or "My zipper's stuck!" or "Mary says I can't borrow her blue

<u>sweater!</u>", good. Those are problems adults can help with. If you know they exist, there are useful things you can do. If action on them has to be postponed, you can explain that to the child. And you can try to make it clear that "I wish I was *dead*" is way out of proportion for problems of that kind. You could say this:

> "Kids who say 'I wish I was *dead*' when their zipper is stuck will have trouble getting people to pay attention when something's <u>really</u> wrong. You might want to think about that."

Suppose, on the other hand, that the child's answer when you ask why is, "I don't know exactly . . . I just feel really sad." In that case, the sadness should be carefully explored, for as long as it takes, and expert help should be found if needed.

The body language of the child who makes a declaration of this kind is more important than the words. When the child is a stranger, it will be harder to make accurate judgments, but usually the adult will know the child. The task is to compare the body language that goes with "I wish I was *dead*" to the child's *usual* body language. Is this a child whose typical reaction to crises like soggy cereal or chipped nailpolish is wild cries of dismay, hands pressed to the head, floods of tears, and so forth? If so, a dramatic "I WISH I was DEAD!" isn't nearly as serious as a simple "I wish I was dead" without the frills. When the very dramatic version with all the extra stresses comes from a child who usually reacts to problems by withdrawing and being very quiet, that's important. In either case, it's not *safe* to assume that the child heard the line on TV and is just trying it out to see what happens. Take time to find *out*. Here's a possible revision of Dialogue 25; notice the adult's Satir Mode choices.

DIALOGUE 25 REVISITED

Child: "I wish I was dead."

Adult: "Tell me about that, please." (Leveling)

Child: "I don't want to tell you."

Adult: "Sometimes it's hard for kids to talk about things that are bothering them." (Computing)

Child: "Yeah. It is."

Adult: "But it's also hard for people to help if they don't know what's wrong. Maybe you could show me." (Computing; then Leveling.)

Child: "It's in my room."

Adult: "Okay. Let's go look." (Leveling)

And later,

Adult: "Next time that happens, it would be a good idea to just come tell me, without saying that you wish you were dead. You could save that for emergencies; that way, when something serious is wrong, you'll have something left to say." (Leveling)

Child: "Okay."

DIALOGUE 26: "I Won't Live to Grow up Anyway . . ."
Shocking as it is to hear this from a child, many children in our big cities now live in such bad situations that the line "I won't live to grow up anyway" makes sense. If you apply Miller's Law, the statement would be true in a world where human beings have a good chance of being shot or stabbed to death while they're still children — and that may well describe the child's situation. As with the sixteen-year-old boy in this dialogue:

Adult: "You're not going to graduate if you keep on cutting class. And that's going to make it hard to get a job."

Teen: "Why should I worry about stuff like that? I won't live to grow up anyway."

Adult: "If you make up your mind that way, you're likely to get careless — maybe not pay attention out on the street like you ought to."

Teen: "I hadn't thought about that . . . you're probably right."

Adult: "So pretend you'll die in your bed at eighty-six, okay? It's safer."

Teen: "Yeah. I'll keep that in mind."

This dialogue is Leveling going both ways, in a situation where both people involved know they live in a hard cold world and nobody has any magic on hand to fix it. Notice that the adult doesn't argue with the boy or challenge his view of reality, and the adult doesn't *preach*. Nothing like, "Maybe you <u>would</u> live to grow up if you'd spend more time in <u>school</u> and less time hanging around on <u>street</u> corners!"

The dialogue is friendly; apparently these two get along pretty well, and the boy doesn't react negatively. But suppose things aren't that ideal, and the adult has reason to believe that caution is needed. What then? In that case, a switch to Computing would be a wise move. For instance:

DIALOGUE 26 REVISITED

Adult: "People who cut class have a hard time graduating— and then they have a hard time getting a job."

(*Note:* "People" is safest here. A defensive young male living in an urban combat zone won't go for "boys" or "kids" or "youngsters." "People" is entirely neutral.)

Teen: "I don't worry about stuff like that; I won't live to grow up anyway."

Adult: "Somebody that makes up his mind that way is likely to get careless — maybe not pay attention out on the street like he ought to."

Teen: "Huh . . . maybe. Maybe so."

Adult: "He might be safer pretending he'll die in his bed at eighty-six — and would rather die with both his legs still attached and still working."

Teen: "Yeah. I hear you."

And when the child is middle-class and living in a pleasant suburb or a little country town? That doesn't mean that "I won't live to grow up" is just melodramatics. Not today. Not in today's United

States, where the gangs are spreading over the country like crabgrass, where AIDS is rampant and tuberculosis is making a strong comeback, and where violence is the most common cause of death before roughly the age of twenty-five. Let's assume that the child comes to you knowing that you're somebody who listens and somebody it's safe to talk to. *Talk it over.* Find out what's going on.

Suppose the child says, "They told us in school today . . . <u>three times</u> as many kids died of AIDS this year as last year! And you can get it even if you're <u>straight</u>!" Then you should say, "Let's talk about it," and if you get turned down, you should keep trying. (Or ask for help from somebody with a better chance of getting through.) The adult in Dialogues 26 and 26 Revisited is right: *When people think there's no hope, they stop being careful.* A teenager convinced that there's no way to keep from getting AIDS won't see any point in trying, and that's very dangerous, for the child and everyone around him. That "I won't live to grow up" attitude leads youngsters straight to just one conviction: *Anything goes, because you have to grab everything right now, while you still have a chance.*

For adults who want to say something positive in a situation like this, I recommend "We're going to do everything possible to make sure you <u>do</u> live to grow up. I promise." It's good to hear an adult say that, even when it's not someone with a lot of power to change the circumstances. The metamessage is: "Lots of kids don't make it; you're right. I won't pretend that that's not the way it is. But I'm on your side, and you can count on me to do whatever I <u>can</u> do."

What You Should Never—Ever—Say

Things that should *not* be said include at least these five, and anything like them:

1. "Oh, don't be riDICulous! You're only trying to get aTTENtion!"

2. "Oh, don't <u>say</u> that! I can't stand to hear you <u>say</u> that! That's <u>horr</u>ible!"

3. "Hey — you watch your <u>mouth</u>!"

4. "There are kids that have <u>real</u> problems, buddy — you should just thank your lucky <u>stars</u> you're not <u>one</u> of them!"

5. "Oh, quit WHINing!"

If you can be *positive* that there's no valid reason for "I won't live to grow up anyway," and you're tired of what you know is only an attempt to manipulate you, you can say this:

"There've got to be better things you could say to let me know you're frustrated about something. Please don't say that line to me again. It's inconsiderate, it's rude, and it upsets people."

DIALOGUE 27: "Because I'm <u>Fat</u> — <u>That's</u> Why!"

Adults know that sometimes you have to lie to children. There are the untruths based on cultural myths, like Santa Claus and the Easter Bunny. Depriving small children of those myths sets them off from their peers and makes them "different" in a way that will almost certainly cause problems. (And puts the adult in a bind . . . how do you explain why all the other adults are lying?) Sometimes we lie to children because the truth is more than a child could handle: This is the "Everything's going to be all right" lie, which we may feel obliged to tell even when we suspect that it's *not* going to be all right. Most of us will agree on what untruths fall into these two groups, and when they're appropriate. For most adults, the arguments about lying to children come up when we get to what are called "white" lies. We teach children that they may *not* tell grownups unpleasant truths about their appearance, even in response to a direct question. A child who answers her grandmother's, "Well, sweetheart, how do I look?" with "Your face is all wrinkled and your dress is too tight" — even if she is speaking the truth — will be in trouble, and most children over the age of three or four understand that.

The question, then, is whether adults should lie to children in similar situations after the children are old enough to make reliable judgments, as in this dialogue with a child of ten.

Adult: "I don't understand. You've been talking about this party for weeks—I heard you talking to somebody about it on the phone only last night. And now you say you aren't going! Why?"

Child: "Because I'm <u>fat</u>—<u>that's</u> why!"

Adult: "Oh, honey, don't be ridiculous! You are <u>not</u> fat!"

Child: "I am <u>so</u>! All the kids call me 'Blob' and 'Fatty' and 'Tubby' . . . I <u>am</u> fat! I'm a <u>freak</u>! And I'm not GOing to their stupid party!"

Adult: "Tracy, look at me. <u>Look</u> at me, and listen to what I'm saying! You are <u>not</u> fat. Never mind what the kids say—they'll say <u>anything</u> that they think will get to you. You are a strong, healthy, husky child; you have big bones. But you are <u>not fat</u>."

Child: "Are <u>you</u> <u>sure</u>?"

Adult: "Cross my heart. Now you'd better hurry and start getting ready for the party, or you'll be late!"

Child: "Okay!"

This adult means well. This is an adult who, looking at a friend's latest bad painting, politely says that it's very interesting. If the child in the dialogue is only a few pounds heavier than the current ideal weight and is exaggerating the problem (as do many dieting-obsessed American adults), then the parent is right and the dialogue represents successful communication.

But suppose it's not like that. Suppose the child is much heavier than what the American mainstream culture specifies as normal weight. Suppose the parent agrees with the other kids that the child is too fat. In that case, Tracy *has* been lied to. And we know that sooner or later—probably sooner—the child will find that out. In that situation, the adult has made a mistake. Tracy is happier right now, but very soon the parent is going to hear "You <u>lied</u> to me! I <u>am</u> fat, and <u>you</u> <u>know</u> it!" Then what? How about this line?

Adult: "You're right; I wasn't being completely truthful with you. But it was because I <u>love</u> you, Tracy, and I didn't want to <u>hurt</u> you!"

The problem with this is its metamessage. It says, loud and clear: "Being fat is so terrible that I was willing to lie to keep you from knowing that it applies to you!" It tells the child that although the adult would never use hurtful names like "Fatty" and "Tubby," the adult also thinks that a body heavier than the ideal is something to be ashamed of. It paves the way for a lifetime of feeling like an outcast—a perception that we all know our mainstream culture will reinforce a dozen times a day. Bias against fat people is one prejudice that our culture not only tolerates but actually *supports*. People who would be disgusted by a magazine cover that showed the national debt as a disabled person in a wheelchair make no objection when the illustration shows a *fat* person in that role.

No matter how irrational this fat prejudice and phobia is—and I think it's *totally* irrational—adults can't wave a magic wand and make it go away. It's *there*, like the bias against very short people and people perceived as ugly. Children *will* have to face it. This is what makes some parents panic and put their tiny kids on dangerous diets. It's what makes them say things like these:

"If you REALLY wanted people to like you, you'd STOP eating like a little PIG and lose that WEIGHT!"

"No matter HOW fat you are, sweetheart, WE love you more than anything else in the WORLD!"

"Either go on a diet and start EXercising, or stop whining and be a happy FAT person—one or the OTHer! It's up to you."

"Okay, so you're fat. So what? You're the smartest kid in your class. When all the skinny kids are on welfare, you'll be able to laugh at them."

"Only lazy greedy people are fat. Think about that!"

All of these utterances, even the ones that are meant to be kind, support the idea that something is terribly *wrong* with the overweight child. And unlike the situation with the child who is short or homely, the grownups aren't saying, "But it's not your fault and there's absolutely nothing you can do about it." Overweight is perceived by most people (and often by overweight people themselves) as a *moral failure*. No amount of scientific research demonstrating that this is false seems to change that perception. Which means that the adult in Dialogue 27 is doing the child no favor. Let's consider a revision:

DIALOGUE 27 REVISITED

Adult: "I don't understand. You've been talking about this party for weeks — I heard you talking to somebody about it on the phone only last night. And now you say you aren't going! Why?"

Child: "Because I'm <u>fat</u>, <u>that's</u> why!"

Adult: "Oh . . . I understand. That's a problem."

Child: "The other kids call me names, Mama — 'Fatty' and 'Tubby' and 'Blob.' Stuff like that."

Adult: "I know. And that makes it really hard for you."

Child: "It's not <u>fair</u>!"

Adult: "No. It's not."

Child: "What do <u>you</u> think I should do?"

Adult: "I think you should go to the party. I think people who judge other people by their shape are ridiculous, and I don't think you should arrange your life to suit <u>them</u>. But I know it's hard to have a good time when the other kids tease you. You don't have to go if you'd rather stay home."

Child: "<u>Some</u> of the kids don't tease me. Some of them are my <u>friends</u>."

Adult: "That's right."

Child: "I think I'll go."

Adult "Then you'd better start getting ready, or you'll be late."

Child: "Okay!"

It might not end like this. It might end with the child saying, "I think I'll stay home," and the adult saying, "That's fine. It's your choice, and I'm 100 percent behind you, either way." Whichever it is, the adult hasn't *lied* to the child this time, or said anything that backs up the bias against overweight. Perhaps most important of all, the adult has shown the child that being fat isn't something so terrible that it *has* to be lied about. It's just a problem you discuss, like many other problems in a world that even a child of nine will have learned is *not* fair.

If you have a child who knows that others see him or her as unattractive, you have to decide for yourself just how much truth that child can handle. There are no hard and fast rules. But it's true that we weave a tangled web when we try to deceive. At best, lying only postpones the moment when the truth will have to be faced. If you feel that it's best to lie, plan ahead for the time when the lie has to be given up.

It's easy to tell a child, "Yes, Johnny, it's true—there's no Santa Claus. But little kids have a lot of <u>fun</u> thinking Santa's real, and when you were little we wanted you to have fun, too. Now that you're a big kid, it's okay for you to know the truth—just don't tell any <u>little</u> kids!" You're welcoming the child into a loving conspiracy when you say that; it's a rite of passage. There's no such positive side to having to admit that you lied about a child's appearance.

Unless it's one of the Easter Bunny lies, or unless you genuinely have no choice, don't lie to children. Say something true instead. Kids are *experts* when it comes to spotting body language that makes words false.

DIALOGUE 28: "I'm Pregnant." (with a fifteen-year-old girl)

The other communication problems discussed in this book have been gender neutral, equally likely to involve male and female youngsters. This next problem, however, can happen only to a girl-child: The problem of saying she's pregnant. (Our society still makes little effort to involve the boys who are the fathers; we still say that girls "get" pregnant, as if they do it all by themselves.) Families do exist where the idea that teenage girls will bear children and raise them without fathers is accepted calmly, but they're rare. For most families, a dialogue like the one below (usually between a mother and daughter) is a shattering and tragic experience.

Teen: "Mom, I have to tell you something."

Adult: "Okay . . . What is it?"

Teen: "I'm sorry. I'm so <u>sorry</u>!"

Adult: "What <u>is</u> it? What's <u>wrong</u>?"

Teen: "Mom, I'm pregnant."

Adult: "Oh, no . . . please, NO!"

Teen: (*Staring at the floor.*) "I said I was sorry."

Adult: "Oh, no . . . I can't believe this! I can't believe it, do <u>you</u> <u>hear</u> <u>me</u>? How could you <u>do</u> this to us? How could you <u>possibly</u> DO this? Do you understand what you have DONE TO US? Do you have ANY idea what you've DONE?"

Teen: "Yeah. I've made the mistake of telling <u>you</u>, THAT'S what I've done!"

Nothing could be more natural than the horror this adult feels. Adults know what comes *next*. There are only three choices: The child has an abortion; the child has the baby and keeps it to bring up; the child has the baby and gives it up for adoption. Each of those choices carries heavy penalties for the pregnant teen, her family, and the baby. There is no *good* choice, and none harder to make. Our language reveals the confusion we feel: We don't even have a word that *works* in this terrible situation. To say "the pregnant child" is absurd; "the pregnant girl" is traditional, but "girl" is wrong too. A pregnant female human being is no longer a girl, but when she's not yet an adult woman, "the pregnant woman" doesn't fit either.

I do not for one minute want to minimize the pain the adult feels. But this is one time when adults must *be* adults and find the strength to set aside their own pain and attend immediately to the child. *If that's not done, everything about their communication from*

*that moment on will be twice as hard, and the harm done will com-
pound the tragedy.* No matter which choice they make, the adults
and the youngster have to establish a foundation of trust, so that
they'll be able to sit down together and discuss the hard decisions
ahead. If that trust is destroyed by the adult's first reaction (as in
Dialogue 28), rebuilding it will take extraordinary skill, at a time
when all the family's resources will already be overextended.

This doesn't mean that the adult has to coddle the erring child.
Whatever our moral position on unmarried pregnancy may be,
except in cases of rape and incest the child *has* helped create a
tragedy, through weakness or carelessness or both. But the adult
needs to remember this:

✦ You have a lifetime ahead of you to make it absolutely clear to
   the child how hurt and angry you are, how disappointed you are,
   how betrayed you feel, how serious the mistake was. That can
   wait.

The message that has to be transmitted right away is, "No matter
how I feel about this, I will do everything I can to keep from making it worse. You're safe with me. We can talk about it." The following dialogue shows a way to do that without sacrificing the dignity or principles of either mother or daughter.

DIALOGUE 28 REVISITED

Teen: "Mom, I have to tell you something."

Adult: "Okay . . . What is it?"

Teen: "I'm sorry. I'm so <u>sorry</u>!"

Adult: "What <u>is</u> it? What's <u>wrong</u>?"

Teen: "Mom, I'm pregnant"

Adult: "You're pregnant?"

Teen: (*Staring at the floor.*) "Yes. I'm sorry, Mom."

Adult: "Thank you for telling me. I know how hard that must have been for you; you knew how I'd feel about it, and how your father would feel. Thank you for coming to me instead of going to somebody outside the family."

Teen: "I was so scared to tell you . . . but I thought, you're my mother. I mean, that's who you tell, when it's something terrible, right? Mom . . . you can yell at me if you want to."

Adult: "No. Let's not have any yelling. Let's sit down and talk about this. And as soon as you're ready to face it, you have to tell your dad. He loves you, too; he won't want to be left out."

If the other parent's reaction would be *literally* dangerous, the teen and the parent she tells first will have one more hard choice to make: Are they going to try to keep the pregnancy a secret from the other parent? And if the teenager can't bring herself to trust either parent and is talking to some other adult entirely, there'll have to be a decision about who to tell next. These are choices that can only be made on a case-by-case basis; there aren't any rules that apply to every pregnant girl and every family.

In all of these situations the adults *must* remember the very real possibility that the teenager will run away or try suicide. Adult pain and anger can trigger those events, as can any action that the child sees as adult treachery.

DIALOGUE 29: "I'm Gay."

The announcement of homosexuality can come from either a male or female child; in the majority of families it will cause the same kind of shock a pregnancy would. Families without negative opinions about homosexuality are no exception—because the adults know how much harder the gay child's life is going to be. (And perhaps because of disappointment over not being able to look forward to grandchildren.) It's like the reaction adults feel when a child announces an intimate relationship with someone of a different race. They're dismayed because they know the consequences the child probably faces as a result of widespread prejudice, whether they feel any prejudice themselves or not. It's very unrealistic, but we adults want the children we care about to have a future free of problems. We're distressed when we hear about any situation that seems to *guarantee* problems for them.

When the adult reaction to "I'm gay" is that the child is no longer part of the family and is banished forthwith, there are no more communication problems — communication is over. But in all other cases the immediate problem is usually how to get through the *first* conversation or two on the subject without saying anything that will make matters worse or do damage that can never be mended, as in the following dialogue between a mother and a seventeen-year-old boy:

Teen: "Mom, there's something I have to tell you — and I know you're not going to like it. Let's just get it over with, okay? Here we go: I'm gay."

Adult: "Oh . . . Are you sure? Are you positive?"

Teen: "Do you think I'd be telling you, if I wasn't?"

Adult: "No. Of course you wouldn't. And I know it wasn't easy for you to decide to tell me; thank you for trusting me."

Teen: "I couldn't go on pretending I wanted to go out with girls, Mom — I couldn't go through with that senior prom scene. I just can't keep on lying."

Adult: "Well . . . It's okay."

Teen: "It's okay? What does that mean, 'it's okay'?"

Adult: "Just what I said. It's okay. Many great men throughout history have been gay. It's no problem. Now — we will never talk about this subject again. Did you take out the trash this morning?"

This adult is *no* good at lying. Obviously, if it's "okay" there's no reason to tell the youngster never to mention the subject again. But parents who are more subtle may believe it's possible for them to pretend a tolerance they don't feel. *That's very unlikely.* Unless the adults have award-caliber acting skills, no matter how carefully they choose their words their body language will betray their true feelings. If they can't *truthfully* say that "it's okay" with them for a child of either gender to be gay, their best course is to speak as honestly as they can, but without abuse, as in this revision of Dialogue 29.

DIALOGUE 29 REVISITED

Teen: "I couldn't go on pretending I wanted to go out with girls, Mom — I couldn't go through with that senior prom scene. I just can't keep on lying."

Adult: "I understand. And I know you won't want me to lie to you, either. You know how I feel about homosexuality. I believe that it's wrong; I won't pretend I don't. We'll just have to work around that, you and I; it doesn't mean I love you any the less. We'll do the best we can."

The most important thing to remember is this:

✦ When you *have to* say something negative, say it as *neutrally* as possible.

"I believe that homosexuality is wrong" is totally negative. But when this is how the adult feels, the child almost certainly already knows it. An adult who feels this way may also feel *morally obligated* to say those words, and — especially if the feeling is based on a religious conviction — to add "and I believe that it's a sin." That's understandable, when it's an honest statement of that person's beliefs and feelings. What *cannot* be justified is saying anything like this: "EVerybody KNOWS it's a SIN, and you MAKE me SICK at my STOMach!" That says to the child, "You're repulsive to me, and you should feel the most profound shame."

Guilt is one thing, shame is another. A gay child, like a pregnant child, may feel guilt about the pain the adult is suffering. Such children may feel guilt because promises have been broken and trust has been betrayed; they may feel guilt about the serious consequences they know are ahead. Someone who accepts guilt can take steps to try to repair the damage and make things right; a person who accepts *shame* will feel that nothing can ever be right again. When shame is added to the equation, the guilt may actually disappear—because the child may feel that the shame pays for the harm that's been done.

Words don't carry shaming messages, but the melody that goes with the words, the intonation of the voice, does. It's unreasonable to expect adults in the situations we've been discussing to suppress their emotions about the things their children have said and done. However, it's not unreasonable to expect them—as the ones with the wisdom and the experience and the power—to *express* those emotions without verbal violence.

DIALOGUE 30: "I'm Hooked."

Like the pregnant or gay child, children who announce that they're addicted must be allowed to keep some dignity; otherwise, communication will be impossible. The adult should thank the child for the trust and courage shown and then should move quickly to do whatever's necessary for the child's safety. Admitting addiction takes exceptional courage, not only because of the negative reaction that's sure to come but because the child knows that the adult will try to cut off all supplies of the addictive substance. The child may want that intellectually and may be actively seeking it for survival's sake; that makes it no less a nightmare.

It's in the adult's own self-interest, whether parent or not, to maintain communication and trust in the addicted child, so that there's some hope of getting the youngster into treatment. We all pay a heavy price for the desperate behavior of addicted persons. We all have to live with the crime and pay the bills for health care, social services, law enforcement, and the criminal justice system. (Not to mention the bill that is beyond all calculation, for lost potential.) Dialogues like this one, between a father and his fourteen-year-old son, will only run those bills higher:

Teen: "Dad . . . I have to tell you something. I'm hooked."

Adult: "You're kidding me."

Teen: "No. I'm really hooked. I need help, Dad."

Adult: "Hooked on what? On <u>what</u>?"

Teen: "Coke. Cocaine."

Adult: "So <u>that's</u> why your grades have gone to hell! And it explains why <u>money</u> keeps disappearing from this house, DOESn't it?"

Teen: "I guess so."

Adult: "You guess so? YOU GUESS SO? Why, YOU little PUNK!"

Teen: "Come on, Dad, I _____"

Adult: "Shut up! Just SHUT UP! And get out of my SIGHT before I break your stupid NECK!"

Teen: "You GOT it!" (*And he's gone.*)

This just plain isn't *smart*. An adult whose reaction to a youngster's confession is that intense and that negative should say this:

Adult: "I hear you. I understand what you're saying. But I don't trust myself to talk about it right now. I need to be by myself a while first. I'm going to go for a walk now, and when I get back, we'll sit down together and talk it over." (*And he's gone.*)

Yes, this is risky. The child may be scared off; the child may leave and not come back. But staying and going through a dialogue like Dialogue 30 *guarantees* those outcomes. With a postponement, there's at least a chance that they won't happen. And on the way out the door the adult should try to find the strength to say, "Thank you for trusting me enough to tell me. I know it wasn't easy."

Movies and television shows give the impression that adults react in only two ways to "I'm pregnant" and "I'm gay" and "I'm hooked." In the media the adults are either unbelievably "cool" and supportive or they're viciously abusive. In the real world, most adults fall somewhere between these two extremes.

DIALOGUE 31: "I'm a <u>Whole</u> <u>New</u> <u>Person</u> Now!"

Problems occur when children announce that they've become members of a religious group (or perhaps an organization or a social movement) that the adult strongly objects to. The issue of belief systems is extremely personal, and the range is broad — one person's cult is another's beloved faith. To avoid making judgments of that kind myself, I'm going to *invent* a group to use in the dialogues. Let's assume that the teenager in the following dialogue has joined a small religious group known as "the Maklunites," whose religious practices would seem very strange to most Americans.

Teen: "Mom . . . There's something I have to tell you."

Adult: "Okay. What is it?"

Teen: "It's wonderful news! Mom, I've become a Maklunite!"

Adult: "Oh, come off it! That's ridiculous! Everybody knows the Maklunites are completely nuts!"

Teen: (*Silence.*)

Adult: "Well?"

Teen: "I don't have anything else to say to you, Mother."

Adult: "Well, what kind of an attitude is that?"

It's a *reasonable* attitude, of course. Youngsters have a hard time bringing up serious matters in conversation with adults in the best of circumstances. If the response to their attempts is instant ridicule (or the "Isn't that cute?" sort of response), they'll back off immediately and stop talking. So would you, in their place.

If you ask most people what the *hardest* topic to discuss with others is, religion will be a common answer; between adults and children, it's even more difficult. For most people in the mainstream American culture, even devout people, it's a social blunder to say anything much beyond an offhand "I'm a Presbyterian" or "I'm Catholic." Often an adult's negative reaction to a child's utterances about religion is caused mostly by embarrassment and lack of practice. One way to manage that embarrassment is to switch *immediately* to Computer Mode. For example:

DIALOGUE 31 REVISITED

Teen: "Mom . . . There's something I have to tell you."

Adult: "Okay. What is it?"

Teen: "It's wonderful news! Mom, I've become a Maklunite!"

Adult: "People say the Maklunites have some interesting ideas."

Teen: "Wait till I tell you, Mom! I'm a whole new person— it's a whole new <u>world</u>!"

Adult: "When a child is happy, parents are usually happy too."

Teen: "Mom, did you know that the Holy One loves you? Loves you unconditionally, no matter how much you've sinned? And forgives you <u>everything</u>?"

Adult: "Forgiveness isn't easy to find, and unconditional love is even rarer."

The mother is just making one innocuous statement after another. Her goal is to keep the conversation going until she gets over the shock of hearing "I've become a Maklunite!" Computer Mode gives her things she can safely say for that purpose. Nothing she's saying—as long as it's said neutrally, not sarcastically or patronizingly—could be hurtful to the child or frighten him into silence. None of it is anything a reasonable person would argue about. It just holds the adult's place in conversational space while the teenager goes on talking and she figures out what approach to take to the situation.

In any interaction with a child that an adult finds embarrassing, a switch to Computer Mode provides distance and helps the adult to keep from saying things that would cause a communication break-down. The mother in the dialogue may be positive that this associa-tion with the Maklunites is just like the child's earlier ambition to become a professional snake charmer, but she is wise to keep that to herself. There are two things that will swiftly and surely turn a child's tentative association into passionate devotion: One is a direct order to give it up, and the other is ridicule. Both should be avoided while you investigate the situation and get more information. Unless the child is in immediate danger, the wisest move is to use Computing to postpone *real* discussion until you're sure what needs to be done.

Talking to the Cyberchild

When a child wants another few dollars' allowance or a new toy, it's usually trivial. But when *cyber*kids start spending money, it can be very large sums, with serious consequences for the family budget. Let's look at two typical dialogues.

DIALOGUE 32: "It's Only Money!"

Teenager: "I don't understand why you say I can't have a new Mac! It's only money — you make <u>plenty</u> of money!"

Adult: "I do pretty well, sure, but I don't get to <u>keep</u> all of it, you know. My expenses are <u>incredible</u>."

Teen: "Yeah? Why?"

Adult: "Rent and overhead for the office costs me a hundred thousand a year and change, for starters."

Teen: "Well, that's just <u>stupid</u>!"

Adult: "You can't do business without _____"

Teen: "Wait! Wait a minute! <u>Nobody</u> needs stuff like that anymore. It went out with the dinosaurs. All you need is a <u>virtual</u> office, don't you know that?"

Adult: "What's a 'virtual' office?"

Teen: "Everybody has their own laptop and modem and you do everything online! What do you need <u>rooms</u> and <u>rugs</u> and stuff like <u>that</u> for?"

Adult: "Oh, come on — I couldn't run a business that way! You've been reading too much science fiction."

Teen: "<u>Sure</u> you could! I'll show you. And since you'd save probably seventy-five thousand a year, can I <u>please</u> have a new Macintosh?"

DIALOGUE 32A: "It's Only Money!" (Again)

Child: "But you <u>can't</u> shut me down! This is my whole life! You can't DO that!"

Adult: "Yes, I can, and I will. We made a deal — I'd pay the ten-bucks-a-month basic charge for you to be online, and <u>you</u> would pay everything else. Remember?"

Child: "I'll be more careful — I promise! Just give me one more chance!"

Adult: "<u>No.</u> This month's phone bill was the last straw. No more cyberspace for you, and that's final. If the real world isn't good enough for you, you can watch *Star Trek!*"

Child: "Hey, cyberspace <u>is</u> the real world! Like <u>you're</u> a vanishing species, you know? The message just hasn't gotten to your <u>brain</u> yet!"

Both of these dialogues show a youngster who is at ease with all the latest technology and comfortable talking about it, and an adult who isn't. When kids talk this way about cars or clothes or most other material things, adults can hold their own. But the adult who still sees computers as nothing but fancy typewriters and calculators isn't equipped for cybertalk. There are only two ways to deal this kind of communication gap.

1. The adult decides to make a genuine effort to learn enough about the youngster's world to at least carry on a competent conversation.

Suppose the adult in Dialogue 32A makes this decision. Then the next few lines would go like this:

Adult: "You made an agreement and you didn't keep it; that's a fact, and it has consequences I can't change. But I don't like making decisions when I don't have enough information. Before I shut you down, I want you to show me <u>why</u> this is so important to you. You help me try out a bulletin board myself, so I can see what it's like. And give me a couple of issues of that magazine you're always reading, ones you think will fill in some of the gaps for me."

Child: "You've gotta be kidding—you'd HATE it!"

Adult: "Maybe. Let's find out. I'm willing to give <u>you</u> a chance, you should give <u>me</u> one. That's fair."

2. The adult has no intention of exploring the youngster's world and makes that absolutely clear, so there can be no question about it. Like this:

Adult: "I understand that this cyberspace world is important to you. <u>You</u> have to understand that it doesn't interest me, and that's not going to change. When you're on your own, the amount of time and money you spend online will be up to you, and I'll respect that. For now, I'm the one paying the bills and the decision is mine. I'll give you one more month. When you show me that I can trust you to pay for the extra hours, you can trust <u>me</u> to keep the account open. Otherwise, I'm shutting it down. That's fair."

Both of these strategies are valid, both are honest, and in both of them the adult is *Leveling* with the child. The temptation to start Blaming in situations like these—to rant and rave about young people's failings, to show contempt for the child's interests and activities, to give orders, to "talk sense"—is very strong, and easy to understand. *Resist it.* When the communication gap is this wide and this deep, you can't build a bridge across it with hostile language.

♦

CHAPTER 7

Conclusion

You've stayed with me now from beginning to end. I am absolutely confident that you can now handle the multitude of communication problems you face with children from toddlers to teens — including convincing them to chew with their mouths shut and hold the cat right side up. I want to close the book by leaving you with five broad guidelines for putting your new information and skills to use.

1. Always remember that your language behavior is the model that the youngsters you interact with use to learn *their* language behavior.

Often this won't be obvious on the surface. You may feel that the children around you are as different from you as rabbits are from seals. But if you're someone constantly present in their language environment, even children who "wouldn't be caught DEAD!" using your slang or wearing your clothes or otherwise copying you will still acquire *your* language strategies — your methods for handling conflict, for getting your way, for persuading others, and so on. The child will also acquire your *nonverbal* communication system, which carries almost all the emotional information and does most of the communication *work*. This gives you an awesome power, both to help and to harm. Use it wisely.

2. Don't lecture children to teach them something; model it instead.

The temptation is always just to *tell.* It's quick and easy to say to a child, "What Bill just said to you was an example of a verbal attack pattern. Here's what you should say back _____" It's quick and easy to say, "The reason you're having trouble communicating with your math prof is because you're touch dominant and she's sight dominant. Here's how you fix it _____" It's harder and slower to make sure your own language behavior models the principles and techniques the kids need to know — and to give them plenty of opportunities to see you *demonstrating* those principles and techniques. It's also much more likely to succeed.

In emergencies, when speed is the most important thing and there's no time to worry about the niceties, you may have to just say "This is how you do it. Say <u>this</u> _____" When a child asks you a direct question about the way you communicate, you *should* answer with explicit instruction and explanation. But always remember that that's not how language learning happens, not for youngsters.

You never told your children, "This is how you make an English yes/no question: Take the first auxiliary verb and move it to the immediate left of the surface subject position in the sentence." They learned how yes/no questions are made by observing the examples all around them and using their innate ability to figure out the rule from the raw data. They learned it so well that they'll never have to think about it again. The best way to teach kids communication is to provide the data and let them work out the rules on their own, so that they will internalize them the same way they internalized all the other rules of their grammar.

3. Do everything you can, honorably and within reason, to prevent loss of face — for everybody involved in any language interaction.

When somebody is made to lose face — by sarcasm, by putdowns, by open abuse, by verbal trickery, by teasing, by shaming — it teaches only one lesson: I'M MORE POWERFUL THAN YOU ARE, THIS TIME. That's rarely a useful lesson, and it doesn't lead to productive communication. It has two predictable consequences: (1) The person who loses face will resent it and remember it and wait for an opportunity to return the favor, or (2) will resent it and remember it and go take that hostility out on somebody else. Or both.

Toxic language is like cholera . . . it spreads from person to person, contaminating and doing harm. If we couldn't avoid that—if there were lots of situations where no tool for communication existed *except* hurtful language—we'd just have to accept it. It would be part of the built-in negatives of human life, like death and taxes. But that's not the way it is. *No matter how negative the content of a message is, there is always a nonabusive way to* <u>transmit</u> *that message.*

4. Try not to lie.

Sometimes you have to lie; that's the nature of the world. Sometimes there are things that have to be hidden from children; sometimes there are social falsehoods (like Easter Bunnies) that you can't avoid. But most of the time, *there is something true that you could say instead of the lie.* Lying is dangerous because children who discover that you've lied to them won't believe you from then on. Lying is dangerous because no matter how carefully you choose your words your body language will betray you. Even the child who doesn't know exactly what the lie *is* will sense that something's going on behind the scenes, and that destroys trust. Before you tell a child a lie that isn't an Easter Bunny or emergency lie, ask yourself, *What true thing could I say instead?*

5. Listen when the child talks, and show the child how good listening is done, every chance you get.

Much of our difficulty in communicating is the result of not listening. Of deciding in advance what someone is going to say and responding to *that* instead of to what's actually said. Of deciding in advance that what someone is going to say isn't worth our time and our attention. Good listening is the cornerstone of good communication. A child who doesn't say much and doesn't say it very well, but who is a good listener, is going to get ahead in this world. Good listeners are rare, and they are highly prized by everyone who knows them.

Sometimes people say something like this to me: "But you're trying to teach me to lie, to act like somebody I'm not! I am hostile and I do say cross things and mean things and I do lose my temper. That's just the way things are—the kids will just have to learn to live with it!" *They're wrong.* They're free to make that choice if they want to, but it's based on misunderstandings.

Your language behavior isn't like your height. It's much more like your behavior when you're driving: You have substantial control over it and you can change it. You don't have to be a person other people will avoid if they can find a way to do so—which is what happens to verbal abusers and to people whose language habits make talking with them a miserable experience. The system in this book doesn't require you to be someone you aren't, or to sacrifice your own beliefs and principles: *It shows you how you can say what you really think and feel, without doing harm. And very often it allows you, at the same time, to do good.*

When you clean up the physical environment around children, you make it more likely that they—and you—will be healthy and safe. When you clean up their language environment, you are doing *exactly* the same thing. Everybody wins, which is as it should be.

Remember: You don't need a language expert, you *are* a language expert! You now have firm access to the information that *makes* you expert, and you know how to use your knowledge and skills for your own benefit and that of everyone around you. I wish you the very best of luck in your language interactions across the generations.

Additional Resources

Activities and Games

Writing Letters You Don't Mail

Sometimes, even when you understand how a nonabusive language interaction would be put together, even when you agree completely with the principles behind it, it's hard to stop thinking about all the hostile things that you *feel* like saying. You know you'll feel terrible later if you say those things. You know they'll make matters worse. But when you don't do anything with them, they pile up inside your head and fester there, and you keep hearing them over and over in your mind. This is bad for you, for your disposition, and for everyone around you. A reliable way to deal with the problem is to get all the toxic language out of your system by writing it down.

Everything you're tempted to say to the child but know you'd regret later can go in your letter.

"Dear Child . . . You are the meanest and most disgusting nine-year-old girl I have ever known in my entire life. I wish I'd never have to see or talk to you again. I'd like to spank you till you're black and blue."

"Dear Child . . . I don't know what I did wrong to end up with a child like you. You're a <u>stupid</u> child. You don't try. You don't even <u>care</u>. I don't like you; I love you, but I don't like you <u>at</u> <u>all</u>."

That sort of thing. You don't want to say such things out loud and you don't want to find yourself thinking them. Write it all down to get it out of your mind and your spirit. Then destroy it, so that you will be truly rid of it.

If you don't like to write, find a private place and time and make a *tape*, the same way. And then erase the tape, so that it's gone for good.

Keeping a Journal or Diary

You may find it helpful to record unpleasant language interactions in a diary, where you can write down things like these:

1. What the youngster (or you) did or said that set things off

2. How you felt about that

3. What you felt like saying or doing about it

4. What you said or did *instead*

5. What you *wish* you'd said or done

6. Any other comments you have

After a few weeks have gone by, go back and look at what you wrote and bring it up to date. Are you still upset about the interaction? Have there been further developments? Do you think you handled it well or would you like to have done it differently?

Some people enjoy keeping journals, and there's much evidence that it's good for your health. It also gives you a way to keep track of how your communication with children develops and changes over time while providing you with a record that can be useful in dealing with later problems. But if you'd hate journal keeping, don't try to force yourself! If you dread the writing, it will only be another source of tension and you're likely to end up blaming the *children* for it.

Television Mode Lotto

Explicit teaching-and-preaching about communication to your own kids is rarely a good idea. But you may be in a role where you have a chance to teach *other* people's children — as a schoolteacher, a youth worker, a youth group leader, and so forth. In that case, Television Mode Lotto (suggested to me by Rebecca Haden, personal communication) is an excellent game to use. It's played by one television set and any number of children.

Give each child a sheet of paper with a grid on it, and write the name of a language behavior mode at the beginning of each horizontal line. For a sensory mode game, draw a five-by-five grid and label the horizontal rows *Sight, Hearing, Touch, Taste,* and *Smell.* For a Satir Mode game, use a four-by-five grid labeled *Blaming, Placating, Computing,* and *Leveling.* (Distracting is so rare that the game would drag on and on, and it's only a combination of the other modes anyway.) To play, the kids watch television, and every time they hear somebody use an example of one of the modes they put a check in the box beside that category. The first child to fill all the spaces in a row wins. (To make the game harder, combine the two grids into one, or make the grids larger.)

Note: Children who can't read can still play this game if they're old enough to understand the categories. You can draw an eye, ear, hand, mouth, and nose for the sensory modes, and use cartoon faces with appropriate expressions for the Satir Modes. Use a scowl for Blaming, an exaggerated smile for Placating, a blank face for Computing, and a relaxed expression for Leveling.

Language Behavior Bee

Another game to use with children (also suggested to me by Rebecca Haden, personal communication) is played like a spelling bee. The children stand in a row, and the adult calls out instructions — prepared in advance, written on slips of paper, and thoroughly shuffled — like "Sight Mode sentence!" or "Computer Mode sentence!" A child who can't supply what's called for, or who repeats an earlier example, has to sit down. The last child standing is the winner. (For a harder game, give instructions such as "Here's a Blamer sentence; say it in Computer Mode" or "This is an example of a verbal attack pattern; give me a response.")

Sources for Commercial Games

If you want to buy board games and related items that teach communication skills, I recommend two sources:

1. Animal Company Games
   P. O. Box 485
   Healdsburg, CA 95448

2. Childswork/Childsplay Center for Applied Psychology, Inc.
   P. O. Box 1586
   King of Prussia, PA 19406

And of course I recommend the computer!

Suggested Reading

1. *How to Talk So Kids Will Listen and Listen So Kids Will Talk* by Adele Faber and Elaine Mazlish. New York: Avon Books, 1980.

   This is a wonderful book, primarily for parents, which is also useful for anyone taking care of children. Faber and Mazlish don't mention the Satir Modes, but many of the tactics they describe are ways of putting things you say to children into Computer Mode instead of Blaming or Placating. Much sensible and useful advice; great comic strips too! (I also recommend their *Liberated Parents/Liberated Children* and *Siblings Without Rivalry,* as well as the audio versions of these books.)

2. *People Skills: How to Assert Yourself, Listen to Others, and Resolve Conflicts* by Robert Bolton, Ph.D. Englewood Cliffs, NJ: Prentice-Hall, 1979.

   This book is one of the very best introductory books on the most basic communication skills. It has a great deal of material on using three-part messages. Though not directed specifically at improving communication across generations, it's extremely useful for that purpose.

3. *How to Say Hard Things the Easy Way* by Richard Walters. Dallas: Word Publishing, 1991.

This is another book for improving communication in general rather than specifically between adults and youngsters. However, it focuses on a wide variety of situations that are likely to come up when you're communicating with children — especially teenage children — and offers very good advice.

4. *Counseling the Culturally Different: Theory & Practice,* 2nd ed., by Derald Wing Sue and David Sue. New York: John Wiley & Sons, 1990.

If your linguistic contact is with children from varying ethnic groups, you need good solid information about their cultures and how they differ in communication terms from mainstream Anglo cultures. This book is a reliable source of such information. It's directed at counselors, but it's not technical and can profitably be used by anyone who interacts with minority youngsters. It includes special sections on counseling Native Americans, Asian Americans, African Americans, and Hispanics.

5. Write or call for the *Chinaberry Catalogue:* 2780 Via Orange Way, Suite B, Spring Valley, CA 91978; telephone: (619) 670-5200.

This is nothing like your usual book catalog! It gives you long, thorough, detailed reviews of books for children and for interacting with children from many different publishers. The catalog is quarterly, runs to more than a hundred pages, divides up the reviews by age level and subject, and has indexes to help you find what you need immediately. If you're looking for books to help you communicate with youngsters about difficult topics — religion, money, sex, puberty, disabilities, racial and other prejudice, aging, marriage and divorce — this catalog is like having your own personal expert librarian on twenty-four-hour duty.

6. For a complete list of products and services available in the *Gentle Art of Verbal Self-Defense* system presented in this book, write to Elgin, Ozark Center for Language Studies, P. O. Box 1137, Huntsville, AR 72740–1137. Call us at (501) 559-2273 during regular business hours, or send e-mail to ocls@sibylline.com.

7. For access to the latest surveys about children, research about children, and the like, write for information to the Children's Defense Fund, 25 E Street Northwest, Washington DC 20001, and request a catalog of its publications. CDF is the leading organization of its kind and a superb source.

8. For excellent material on the subject of children (including cyberkids) and money, I recommend *Kiplinger's Money-Smart Kids,* from The Kiplinger Washington Editors, Inc., 1729 H Street NW, Washington, DC 20006.

9. Most of the magazines on interacting with children seem to me to have the children of 1950s households in mind instead of today's kids. For a better source of information and ideas, subscribe to *Family Life,* from P. O. Box 52212, Boulder, CO 80321–2212.

10. If you feel that your child might need expert help or counseling, I suggest reading "Therapy for Children," by K. D. Fishman, *Atlantic Monthly,* June 1991, pp. 47–81. Fishman carefully discusses all the major types of therapy for children, comparing and contrasting them, discussing their merits and drawbacks, and so forth.

The Gentle Art
of Verbal Self-Defense:
An Overview

Just as English has a grammar for things like word order and word endings, there's a grammar of English for verbal violence and verbal self-defense. All native speakers of English know this grammar, although such things as nervousness, illness, and lack of time interfere with its use in real life. A major source of problems is that the information about how to make this grammar work for you isn't where you can get at it easily. The *Gentle Art* system is designed to help with this.

When you use this system for verbal self-defense, you won't be restricted to sarcastic comebacks and counterattacks. Instead, you will be able to create for yourself a language environment where verbal confrontations will be very rare. And when they do happen, you'll be able to deal with them quickly and competently, with no sacrifice of your own self-respect, and no loss of face on either side.

This section will introduce you briefly to the basic concepts of the *Gentle Art of Verbal Self-Defense* system, with examples of their use.

Four Reference Items

1. The Four Basic Principles

ONE: KNOW THAT YOU ARE UNDER ATTACK.

TWO: KNOW WHAT KIND OF ATTACK YOU ARE FACING.

THREE: KNOW HOW TO MAKE YOUR DEFENSE FIT THE ATTACK.

FOUR: KNOW HOW TO FOLLOW THROUGH.

The first principle is important because many verbal victims aren't aware that they are victims. Typically, they feel miserable but they don't know why, and they tend to blame not those who abuse them but themselves. For English, the most important clue for knowing that a verbal attack is taking place is not the words being said but the intonation of the voice that's saying them — the "tune" the words are set to.

The second and third principles work together to help you tailor your responses. When you learn to recognize language behavior modes and to put together responses based on rules for their use, you're applying these two principles.

The fourth principle is often the hardest. There are two barriers to its use: (1) the idea that if you don't participate in the power game of verbal abuse, you're letting the abuser "get away with it," and (2) the problem of feeling guilty about defending yourself. Both of these barriers are based on misconceptions. When you play the role of victim in verbal confrontations, you're training your attacker to be a more skilled verbal abuser — you're providing the attacker with practice and encouragement. That's not kind or nurturing. And when you let somebody involve you in verbal violence, that — not the words said — is letting the person get away with it.

2. Miller's Law

In order to understand what another person is saying, you must assume that it is true and try to imagine what it could be true of.

(George Miller, in E. Hall, 1980)

Notice that you don't have to *accept* that it's true — just *assume,* temporarily, that it is. And ask yourself what it could be true *of.* Often what we do is use a kind of "Miller's-Law-in-Reverse," where we assume that what's being said is *false* and try to imagine what could be wrong with the *person speaking* that made them say something so outrageous. This guarantees communication breakdown; follow Miller's Law instead.

3. Presupposition

A presupposition is anything that a native speaker of a language knows is part of the meaning of a sequence of that language even when it doesn't appear on the surface.

Every English speaker knows that the meaning of "EVen JOHN could pass THAT course!" includes two more sentences saying that the class is somehow second rate and so is John. The sentence means: "Even John (who, as everybody knows, is no great shakes as a student) could pass that course (which, as everybody knows, is really trivial.)" But the negative comments about John and the course aren't there in the surface structure of the sentence: *They are presupposed.* Most verbal attacks, with the exception of the very crudest ones, are at least partly sheltered in presuppositions.

4. Three-Part Messages

The three-part message is a pattern developed by Dr. Thomas Gordon as a way to bypass the automatic negative reaction adult speakers of English have to commands and complaints and criticism. It looks like this:

When you [X],   I feel [Y],   because [Z].

Each part of the message has to be filled with something that is concrete and verifiable in the real world; ideally it will also be something that no reasonable person would argue about. An example of a perfect three-part message is: "When you don't water the tomatoes, I feel angry, because plants die without water."

First Technique—Using the Sensory Modes

Human beings can't survive without information. We need data from the outside environment and from our bodies; we need data from other human beings and living creatures. Without a system for *managing* all this data, it would be impossible to deal with. Information that's coming in has to be processed. Our primary tool for this processing is the set of sensory *systems* — sight and hearing and touch, taste and smell, and so forth

Each of us has one sensory system that we find easiest to use and that helps us most in understanding and remembering. And when we talk we often demonstrate this preference by using one of the language behavior modes called *sensory modes*. For instance —

Sight: "I really like the way this looks."

Hearing: "This just sounds great to me."

Touch: "I really feel good about this."

People who are relaxed and at ease use all the sensory modes, switching among them without any difficulty. But people who are under stress tend to get locked in to their preferred mode. The more upset they are, the more likely this is. In such situations, you can improve communication dramatically by *matching* the sensory mode the other person is using.

You'll recognize the sensory mode coming at you automatically, just because you speak English. To respond to it, just follow these two simple rules:

✦ RULE ONE: Match the sensory mode coming at you.

✦ RULE TWO: If you can't follow rule one, try to use no sensory language at all.

If someone who's been injured asks, "How bad does it look?," use Rule One and say, "I don't see it as anything serious." Or use Rule Two and say, "In my opinion, it's not serious." Rule Two doesn't give you the same advantages as Rule One, but it's much better than answering the question with, "I don't feel that it's very serious," which is sensory mode *mis*match.

Second Technique—Using the Satir Modes

Dr. Virginia Satir was a world-famous family therapist. As she worked with clients, she noticed that the language behavior of people under stress tends to fall into one of the following five categories, which we call the *Satir Modes*.

BLAMING

"WHY don't you ever think about anybody ELSE's feelings? DON'T you have ANY consideration for other people at ALL?"

PLACATING

"Oh, YOU know how I am!—whatever YOU want to do is okay with ME!"

COMPUTING

"There must be a good reason for this delay. No sensible person would be upset."

DISTRACTING

"WHAT IS THE MATTER with you, ANYway? Not that I care! YOU know me—I can put up with ANYthing! However, common sense would indicate that the original agreement should be followed. And I am really FED UP with this garbage!!"

LEVELING

"I like you. But I don't like your methods."
Each Satir Mode has its own style of body language. Blamers

shake their fists or their index fingers; they scowl and frown and loom over people. Placaters cling and fidget and lean on others. Computer body language is neutral, even monotonous. Distracters cycle through the other modes with their bodies just as they do with their words. Leveler body language is what's left over, and it will match the words the Leveler uses.

The first four Satir Modes are examples of *mismatch* between the message outside and the feelings inside. People use Blaming messages that say, "I have all the power!", but inside they're afraid nobody will respect or obey them. People use Placater Mode—saying that they don't care at all—because they care so very much. They use Computer Mode, saying, "I have no emotions," because they have one or more emotions they're not willing to let show. Distracters don't know what to say, so they say everything they can think of. Only with Leveler Mode (or Computer Mode used deliberately for strategic reasons) do inside and outside *match*. To the extent that they *know* their own feelings and the facts behind them, people using Leveler Mode use words and body language that match those feelings.

As with the sensory modes, people can ordinarily switch from one Satir Mode to the other, but they tend to become locked in to preferred Satir Modes in situations of tension and stress. The rules for using the Satir Modes are based on the metaprinciple, ANYTHING YOU FEED WILL GROW. All language interactions are *feedback loops*. When you match a language pattern coming at you, you feed it and it escalates. The difference between the two techniques is that it's always a good thing to match another person's sensory mode, because it's always good to increase the level of trust and good feeling. But you should only match a Satir Mode if you *want* the behavior it produces to grow.

You'll recognize the Satir Modes automatically because they're part of your grammar. Here are the rules for responding:

✦ RULE ONE: If it would be desirable for the Satir Mode coming at you to escalate, match it.

✦ RULE TWO: If you don't know what to do, go to Computer Mode and stay there until you have a reason to change.

Note: Satir Modes are just language behaviors; they're not part of people's characters or personalities. Nobody "is" a Blamer or Placater. To say, "Blamers do something" is just shorthand for "People who are at that particular moment using the Satir Mode called *Blaming* do something."

Third Technique—
Managing the Verbal Attack Patterns of English

Many people don't realize they are verbal victims because the verbal abuse they encounter isn't *openly* abusive. Most verbal abusers don't just spit out curses and insults. (That sort of behavior is usually part of a pattern of *physical* abuse.) Instead, they rely heavily on the set of verbal attack patterns (VAPs) that are part of the grammar of English verbal violence. These patterns are just as dangerous as shouted obscenities, but much more subtle.

The attack patterns discussed below have two parts. There is the BAIT, which the attacker expects you to respond to. It's easy to recognize, because it's the part that *hurts.* And then there is at least one other attack, sheltered inside a presupposition. Here's an example:

"If you REALLY loved me, YOU wouldn't waste our MONey!"

The bait is "You waste our money." Your attacker expects you to take the bait and say, "What do you MEAN, I waste money! I DO NOT!" And then you're off to a flaming row, which is a poor way to handle the situation. Instead of taking the bait, answer the attack sheltered in "If you REALLY loved me," which means "You don't really love me." Say:

"When did you start thinking that I don't really love you?"

or

"Of course I love you."

This isn't what the attacker expects, and it will shortcircuit the confrontation.

Here are some other examples of English VAPs:

"If you REALLY wanted me to get a job, YOU'D buy me a decent CAR like all the OTHER kids have got!"

"A person who REALLY cared about his health wouldn't WANT to smoke!"

"DON'T you even CARE if you look like a NERD?"

"EVen somebody YOUR age should be able to cook LUNCH!"

"EVerybody underSTANDS why you're so TOUCHY, dear!"

"WHY don't you ever LISTEN to me when I talk to you?"

"YOU'RE not the ONly person with PROBlems, you know!"

It's important to realize that what makes these examples attacks is not the words they contain, but the tune that goes *with* the words. Any time you hear a lot of extra stresses and emphasis on words or parts of words, you should be on the alert, because this is the most important cue for recognizing verbal attacks. The question, "Why do you eat so much junk food?" may be very rude and unkind, but it's not a verbal attack. The attack that goes with those words is "WHY do you eat SO MUCH JUNK food?"

Here are the rules for the verbal attack patterns:

✦ RULE ONE: Ignore the bait.

✦ RULE TWO: Respond directly to a presupposition.

✦ RULE THREE: No matter what else you do, say something that transmits this message: "You're wasting your time trying that with me. I won't play that game."

Nobody can carry on a verbal attack alone. It takes two people — one to be the attacker, and one to be the victim. People who use verbal abuse do so because they want the fight or the scene—they want your *attention*—and they enjoy the havoc they create. When you take the bait in their attacks and go along with their plans, you're giving them *exactly what they want.* Instead of doing that, use this third technique and break out of the loop. That's not "letting them get away with it." Letting them sucker you into giving them your attention on demand and playing verbal victim for them *is.*

Victims of verbal abuse are not helpless to protect themselves. And it's not true that verbal abusers can't change their language behavior, or that doing so will mean sacrificing their self-respect. The *Gentle Art* system is a practical method for tackling the problems of everyone involved in verbal abuse—attackers, victims, and innocent bystanders—with no loss of face or sacrifice of principle.

Pollution in the language environment is just as dangerous as pollution in the physical environment. You can use the *Gentle Art of Verbal Self-Defense* to get rid of almost all of it and to deal skillfully with what remains.

Bibliography

Articles

Addington, D. W. "The Relationship of Selected Vocal Characteristics to Personality Perception." *Speech Monographs* 35 (1968): 492–503.

A. F. G. "Notes: Judges' Nonverbal Behavior in Jury Trials: A Threat to Judicial Impartiality." *Virginia Law Review* 61 (1975): 1266–98.

Albert, M. "Universal Grammar." *Z*, December 1988, pp. 99–104.

Beattie, G. W. "Interruption in Conversational Interaction, and Its Relation to the Sex and Status of the Interactants." *Linguistics* 19 (1981): 15–35.

_____. "The Regulation of Speaker-Turns in Face-to-Face Conversation: Some Implications for Conversation in Sound-Only Communication Channels." *Semiotica* 34 (1981): 55–70.

Bell, C. "Family Violence." *Journal of the American Medical Association,* September 19, 1986, pp. 1501–1502.

Bettelheim, B. "Punishment Versus Discipline." *Atlantic Monthly,* November 1985, pp. 51–59.

Blakeslee, S. "Cynicism and Mistrust Tied to Early Death." *New York Times,* January 17, 1989.

Blanck, P. D. "The Appearance of Justice: Judges' Verbal and Nonverbal Behavior in Criminal Jury Trials." *Stanford Law Review,* November 1985: 89–163.

_____. "Off the Record: Nonverbal Communication in the Courtroom." *Stanford Lawyer,* Spring 1987, pp. 18–23 and 39.

Bolinger, D. "Contrastive Accent and Contrastive Stress." *Language* 37 (1961): 83–96.

Bolles, E. B. "The Intimate Grammar of Baby Talk." *Saturday Review,* March 18, 1972, pp. 52–55.

Brothers, J. "Turn a Drawback into a Strength." *Parade,* April 10, 1994, pp. 4–6.

Check, W. E. "Homicide, Suicide, Other Violence Gain Increasing Medical Attention." *Journal of the American Medical Association,* August 9, 1985, pp. 721–30.

Coles, R. "Listening to Children." *Family Life,* March–April 1994, pp. 48–49.

Cosmides, L. "Invariance in the Acoustic Expression of Emotion During Speech." *Journal of Experimental Psychology,* December 1983, pp. 864–81.

Dimsdale, J. E., MD. "A Perspective on Type A Behavior and Coronary Disease." *New England Journal of Medicine,* January 14, 1988, pp. 110–12.

Douglis, C. "The Beat Goes On." *Psychology Today,* November 1987, pp. 38–42.

Easton, N. J. "It's Cool to Be Cruel: Forget the Niceties, America Is on a Mean Streak." *Dallas Morning News,* July 4, 1993.

Edelsky, C. "Who's Got the Floor?" *Language in Society* 10 (1981): 383–421.

Ervin-Tripp, S., et al. "Language and Power in the Family." In C. Kramerae et al., eds., *Language and Power* (Beverly Hills, CA: Sage Publications, 1984), pp. 116–35.

Fellman, B. "Talk: The Not-So-Silent Killer." *Science* 85 (December 1985): 70–71.

———. "A Conversation with Ira Progoff." *Medical Self-Care,* July–August 1978, pp. 11–12.

Fincher, J. "Inside an Intensive Journal Workshop." *Medical Self-Care,* July–August 1978, pp. 6–10.

Finkbeiner, A. "The Puzzle of Child Abuse." *Science Illustrated,* June–July 1987, pp. 14–19.

Fishman, K. D. "Therapy for Children." *Atlantic Monthly,* June 1991, pp. 47–81.

Foster, D. "The Disease Is Adolescence." *Utne Reader,* July–August 1994, pp. 50–55.

Fox, B. H., Ph.D. "Depression Symptoms and Cancer." *Journal of the American Medical Association,* September 1, 1989, p. 1231.

Franklin, D. "Charm School for Bullies." *Hippocrates,* May–June 1989, pp. 75–77.

Friedman, M., MD. "Type A Behavior and Mortality from Coronary Heart

Disease." *New England Journal of Medicine,* July 14, 1988, p. 114. (See also other letters under same title, through p. 117.)

Gillespie, N. "Teach Your Children Well." (Review of W. J. Bennett's *The Book of Virtues.) Reason,* December 1994, pp. 57–60.

Gold, P. W., MD, et al. "Clinical and Biochemical Manifestations of Depression: Relation to Neurobiology of Stress," part 1: *New England Journal of Medicine,* August 11, 1988, pp. 348–51; part 2: August 18, 1988, pp. 413–20.

Goldberg, J. "Anatomy of a Scientific Discovery." *Science Illustrated,* January–February 1989, pp. 5–12.

Goleman, D. "Studies Point to Power of Nonverbal Signals." *New York Times,* April 8, 1986.

_____. "Research Affirms Power of Positive Thinking." *New York Times,* February 3, 1987.

_____. "The Mind Over the Body." *New York Times Magazine,* September 27, 1987, pp. 36–39 and 59–60.

_____. "Researchers Find That Optimism Helps the Body's Defense System." *New York Times,* April 20, 1989.

_____. "Researchers Trace Empathy's Roots to Infancy." *New York Times,* April 28, 1989.

_____. "A Feel-Good Theory: A Smile Affects Mood." *New York Times,* July 18, 1989.

_____. "Sensing Silent Cues Emerges As Key Skill." *New York Times,* October 10, 1989.

Granat, D. "Mother Knows Best." *Washingtonian,* November 1992, pp. 41–45.

Gray, F., et al. "Little Brother Is Changing You." *Psychology Today,* March 1974, pp. 42–46.

Greydanus, D. E. "Risk-Taking Behaviors in Adolescence." *Journal of the American Medical Association,* October 16, 1987, p. 2110.

Gutner, T. "Junior Entrepreneurs." *Forbes,* May 9, 1994, pp. 188–89.

Haden, R. "A Comparative Exploration of the Expression of Anger in Fourteen Languages, and Some Implications." *Arktesol Post,* Summer–Fall 1987, pp. 7–10.

Hall, E. "Giving Away Psychology in the 80's: George Miller Interviewed by Elizabeth Hall." *Psychology Today,* January 1980, pp. 37–50 and 97–98.

Hall, S. S. "A Molecular Code Links Emotions, Mind and Health." *Smithsonian Magazine,* June 1989, pp. 62–71.

Harvey, J. B. "The Abilene Paradox: The Management of Agreement." *Organizational Dynamics,* Summer 1974, pp. 1–18.

Higgins, L. C. "Hostility Theory Rekindles Debate Over Type A Behavior." *Medical World News,* February 27, 1989, p. 21.

Hollien, M. "Vocal Indicators of Psychological Stress." *Annals of the New York Academy of Science* 347 (1980): 47–72.

House, J. S., et al. "Social Relationships and Health." *Science,* July 29, 1988, pp. 540–44.

"Image and Likeness" [interview with Bishop Kallistos Ware]. *Parabola,* Spring 1985, pp. 62–71.

Jackson, D. S. "Cyberpunk." *Time,* February 8, 1993, pp. 59–65.

Jones, E. E. "Interpreting Interpersonal Behavior: The Effects of Expectancies." *Science,* October 3, 1986, pp. 41–46.

Kamiya, G. "The Cancer Personality." *Hippocrates,* November–December 1989, pp. 92–93.

Kobasa, S. O. "Test for Hardiness: How Much Stress Can You Survive?" *American Health,* September 1984, p. 64.

Kochakian, M. J. "Those Youngsters Out of Synch." *Gannett Suburban Newspapers,* May 18, 1992.

Kohn, A. "Beyond Selfishness." *Psychology Today,* October 1988, pp. 34-38.

Kotulak, R. "Mind Over Matter." *Calgary Herald,* May 1, 1993.

Krier, B. A. "Conversation Interruptus: Critical Social Skill or Just Plain Rudeness?" *Los Angeles Times,* December 14, 1986.

Lynch, J. J., Ph.D. "Interpersonal Aspects of Blood Pressure Control." *Journal of Nervous and Mental Diseases* 170 (1982): 143–53.

_____. "Listen and Live." *American Health,* April 1985, pp. 39–43.

McConnell-Ginet, S. "Intonation in a Man's World." In B. Thorne et al., eds., *Language, Gender, and Society* (Rowley, MA: Newbury House, 1983), pp. 69–88.

Medvescek, C. R. "Toddler Talk." *Parents Magazine,* December 1992, pp. 73–77.

Miller, S. M. "Why Having Control Reduces Stress: If I Can Stop the Roller Coaster I Don't Have to Get Off." In J. Garber and M. E. P. Seligman, eds., *Human Helplessness: Theory and Applications.* New York: Academic Press, 1989.

Milstead, J. "Verbal Battering," *BBW,* August 1985, pp. 34–35, 61, and 68.

Miron, M. S., and T. A. Pasquale. "Psycholinguistic Analysis of Coercive Communication." *Journal of Psycholinguistic Research* (1985): 95–120.

Orlean, S. "The American Man at Age Ten." *Esquire,* December 1992, pp. 115–28.

Parlee, M. B. "Conversational Politics." *Psychology Today,* May 1979, pp. 45–86.

Pfeiffer, J. E. "Between Us Babies." *Science Illustrated,* June 1987, pp. 27–31.

Phillips, P. "Domestic Violence on the Increase." *Cortlandt Forum,* November 1992, pp. 48DD–48EE.

Pines, M. "Psychological Hardiness: The Role of Challenge in Health." *Psychology Today,* December 1980, pp. 34–45.

Rayl, A. J. S. "Secrets of the Cyberculture." *OMNI,* November 1992, pp. 59–67.

Rothschild, M. "Cro-Magnon's Secret Weapons." *Forbes ASAP,* September 19, 1993, pp. 19–20.

Sacks, H., et al. "A Simplest Systematics for the Organization of Turn-Taking for Conversation." *Language* 50 (1974): 696–735.

Scherwitz, L., et al. "Self-Involvement and the Risk Factors for Coronary Heart Disease." *Advances,* Winter 1985, pp. 6–18.

Seligman, J., et al. "Emotional Child Abuse: Discipline's Fine Line." *Newsweek,* October 3, 1988, pp. 48–50.

_____. "The Wounds of Words: When Verbal Abuse Is As Scary As Physical Abuse." *Newsweek,* October 12, 1992, pp. 90–92.

Seligman, M. E. P. "You Gotta Have Hope . . . ," *Parents Magazine,* December 1992, pp. 92–99.

Shea, M. J., MD. "Mental Stress and the Heart." *Cardiovascular Reviews & Reports,* April 1988, pp. 51–58.

Spock, B. Interview by *Sesame Street Parents Guide,* April 1992, pp. 16–18.

Tavris, C. "Anger Defused." *Psychology Today,* November 1982, pp. 25–35.

Weiner, E. J. "A Knowledge Representation Approach to Understanding Metaphors." *Computational Linguistics* 10 (1984): 1–14.

Wolkomir, R. "We're Going to Have Computers Coming Out of the Woodwork." *Smithsonian Magazine,* September 1994, pp. 82–93.

Wright, H. N. "Toxic Talk." *Christian Parenting Today,* July–August 1991, pp. 24–30.

Zajonc, R. B. "Emotion and Facial Efference: A Theory Reclaimed." *Science,* April 5, 1985, pp. 15–20.

Zal, H.M., DO. "The Psychiatric Aspects of Myocardial Infarction." *Cardiovascular Reviews & Reports,* February 1987, pp. 33–37.

Zimmerman, J. "Does Emotional State Affect Disease?" *MD,* April 1986, pp. 30 and 41–43.

Zonderman, A. B., et al. "Depression as a Risk for Cancer Morbidity and Mortality in a Nationally Representative Sample." *Journal of the American Medical Association,* September 1, 1989, pp. 1191–95.

Books

Ader, R. ed. *Psychoneuroimmunology*. New York: Academic Press, 1981.

Ammerman, R. T., and M. Hersen, eds. *Treatment of Family Violence.* New York: John Wiley & Sons, 1990.

_____. *Assessment of Family Violence.* New York: John Wiley & Sons, 1992.

Argyle, M. *Bodily Communication.* London: Methuen, 1975.

Antonovsky, A. *Health, Stress, and Coping.* San Francisco: Jossey-Bass, 1979.

Barsy, A. J., MD. *Worried Sick: Our Troubled Quest for Wellness.* Boston: Little, Brown, 1988.

Beattie, G. *Talk: An Analysis of Speech and Non-Verbal Behaviour in Conversation.* Milton Keynes, England: Open University Press, 1983.

Blumenthal, M. D., et al. *More About Justifying Violence: Methodological Studies of Attitudes and Behavior.* Ann Arbor: University of Michigan, 1975.

Bolinger, D. *Intonation.* Harmondsworth: Penguin Books, 1972.

_____. *Language: The Loaded Weapon.* New York: Longman, 1980.

_____. *Intonation and Its Parts: Melody in Spoken English.* Stanford, CA: Stanford University Press, 1986.

Bolton, R. *People Skills: How to Assert Yourself, Listen to Others and Resolve Conflicts.* Englewood Cliffs, NJ: Prentice-Hall, 1979.

Bondar, J. *Kiplinger's Money-Smart Kids.* Washington, DC: Kiplinger Washington Editors, 1993.

Burbatti, G. L., and L. Formenti. *The Milan Approach to Family Therapy.* Northvale, NJ: Jason Aronson, 1988.

Chesney, M., and R. H. Rosenman, eds. *Anger and Hostility in Cardiovascular and Behavioral Disorders.* Washington, DC: Hemisphere Corporation, 1985.

Clark, V. P., et al., eds. *Language: Introductory Readings,* 3rd ed. New York: St. Martin's Press, 1981.

Craig, R. T., and K. Tracy. *Conversational Coherence: Form, Structure, and Strategy.* Beverly Hills, CA: Sage Publications, 1983.

Elgin, S. H. *The Gentle Art of Verbal Self-Defense.* New York: Barnes and Noble, 1985. (Originally published by Prentice-Hall, 1980.)

_____. *More on the Gentle Art of Verbal Self-Defense.* New York: Prentice-Hall, 1983.

_____. *Manual for Gentle Art Syntonics Trainers,* vol. 1: *Level One;* vol. 2: *Level Two.* Huntsville, AR: Ozark Center for Language Studies, 1986.

_____. *The Last Word on the Gentle Art of Verbal Self-Defense*. New York: Prentice-Hall, 1987.

_____. *Success with the Gentle Art of Verbal Self-Defense*. Englewood Cliffs, NJ: Prentice-Hall, 1989.

_____. *Mastering the Gentle Art of Verbal Self-Defense*. Englewood Cliffs, NJ: Prentice-Hall, 1989. (Audio program.)

_____. *Staying Well with the Gentle Art of Verbal Self-Defense*. Englewood Cliffs, NJ: Prentice-Hall, 1991.

Ekman, P., et al. *Emotion in the Human Face*. New York: Pergamon, 1972.

Friedman, M., and R. H. Rosenman. *Type A Behavior and Your Heart*. New York: Knopf, 1974.

Gardner, H. *The Mind's New Science: A History of the Cognitive Revolution*. New York: Basic Books, 1985.

Gordon, T. *Leader Effectiveness Training: L.E.T.* New York: Wyden Books, 1972.

Hall, E. T. *The Silent Language*. New York: Doubleday/Anchor, 1959.

_____. *Beyond Culture*. New York: Doubleday/Anchor, 1977.

Justice, B. *Who Gets Sick?: Thinking and Health*. Houston: Peak Press, 1987.

Key, M. R., ed. *The Relationship of Verbal and Nonverbal Communication*. The Hague: Mouton, 1980.

Lakoff, G., and M. Johnson. *Metaphors We Live By*. Chicago: University of Chicago Press, 1980.

Lakoff, R. *Talking Power: The Politics of Language in Our Lives*. New York: Basic Books, 1990.

Lazarus, R. S., and S. Folkman. *Stress, Appraisal, and Coping*. New York: Springer, 1984.

Leech, G. *Principles of Pragmatics*. London: Longman, 1983.

Levy, S. M. *Behavior and Cancer*. San Francisco: Jossey-Bass, 1985.

Locke, S., et al., eds. *Foundations of Psychoneuroimmunology*. New York: Aldine, 1985.

Locke, S., and D. Colligan. *The Healer Within: The New Medicine of Mind and Body*. New York: New American Library/Mentor, 1987.

Lynch, J. J. *The Broken Heart: The Medical Consequences of Loneliness*. New York: Basic Books, 1977.

_____. *The Language of the Heart: The Body's Response to Human Dialogue*. New York: Basic Books, 1985.

Miller, G. A. *The Psychology of Communication*. New York: Basic Books, 1975.

_____. *Spontaneous Apprentices: Children and Language*. New York: Seabury Press, 1977.

_____. *The Science of Words*. New York: Freeman, 1991.

Ornstein, R., and D. Sobel. *The Healing Brain: Breakthrough Discoveries About How the Brain Keeps Us Healthy.* New York: Simon and Schuster, 1987.

Ornstein, R., and C. Swencious. *The Healing Brain: A Scientific Reader.* New York: Guilford Press, 1990.

Pinker, S. *The Language Instinct.* New York: Morrow, 1994.

_____. *Language Learnability and Language Development.* Cambridge, MA: Harvard University Press, 1984.

Postman, N. *Crazy Talk, Stupid Talk: How We Defeat Ourselves by the Way We Talk — and What to Do about It.* New York: Dell, 1961.

Progoff, I. *At a Journal Workshop.* New York: Dialogue House, 1975.

Rainer, T. *The New Diary.* Los Angeles: Jeremy P. Tarcher, 1978.

Renkema, J. *Discourse Studies: An Introductory Textbook.* Philadelphia: John Benjamins, 1993.

Rothwell, J. D. *Telling It Like It Isn't.* Englewood Cliffs, NJ: Prentice-Hall, 1982.

Satir, V. *Conjoint Family Therapy.* Palo Alto, CA: Science and Behavior Books, 1964.

_____. *Peoplemaking.* Palo Alto, CA: Science and Behavior Books, 1972.

Thorne, B., and N. Henley, eds. *Language and Sex, Difference and Dominance.* Rowley, MA: Newbury House, 1975.

Thorne, B., et al., eds. *Language, Gender and Society.* Rowley, MA: Newbury House, 1983.

Van Dijk, T. A., ed. *Handbook of Discourse Analysis.* London: Academic Press, 1985.

Watzlawick, P., et al. *Pragmatics of Human Communication: A Study of Interactional Patterns, Pathologies, and Paradoxes.* New York: Norton, 1967.

Index

189